In the Mountains of Heaven

In the Mountains of Heaven

Tales of Adventure on Six Continents

Mike Tidwell

THE LYONS PRESS
Guilford, Connecticut
An imprint of The Globe Pequot Press

The Lyons Press is an imprint of The Globe Pequot Press.

10 9 8 7 6 5 4 3 2 1

Printed in the United States of America

ISBN 1-58574-627-4

Library of Congress Cataloging-in-Publication Data is available on file.

For my parents,
Wayne and Peggy.

When a child has the confidence to wander far
from home, he's been raised well.
When he has the sense to come back home, he's
been well loved.

Contents

Contents

IV
NORTH OF THE BORDER,
SOUTH OF THE BORDER

V
PLANES, TRAINS, CARS

VI
DEPARTURE

Acknowledgments

More than half the essays in this collection first appeared in the Sunday travel section of the *Washington Post*. That's because Craig Stoltz, former editor of the section, was foolish enough to let me talk him into all manner of story ideas no other editor in America wanted. "We can't do a *travel* story about fishing in Washington, D.C.!" he told me over and over again before finally letting me drag my fishing rod by taxi, bus, and subway through the capital in search of largemouth bass. Craig was no slacker himself, hatching his own harebrained schemes that led me to a seal-inhabited rock twelve thousand miles away in Australia and to a desert island in the Bahamas where I promptly got myself marooned. Thanks, Craig. Writers spend half their lives dreaming of editors like you. Few find them.

Many thanks also to others at the *Post*, including current travel editor extraordinaire K.C. Summers and her first lieutenant, John Deiner. Other editors who first published parts of this collection include Richard Busch at *National Geographic Traveler*, Sherri Dalphonse at *Washingtonian*, and David Arnold at *Worldview*. You are all much appreciated.

Finally, hats off to the usual band of suspects: my wife, Catherine; John Coyne; Kitty Thuermer; Nick Varchaver; Ishen Obolbekov; and all those far-flung strangers on six continents who gave aid large and small to an often tired and confused traveler with a reporter's notebook in his back pocket. You made this book possible.

Introduction

T his collection of essays began with a hitchhiking trip I took with a Laundromat repairman on a snowy Thanksgiving eve in 1981, bouncing from Bozeman, Montana, to Denver, Colorado. I was on my way to visit my uncle Barry who, now that I think about it, is the one responsible for these stories, though he doesn't know it and never will.

I had moved to Montana at age nineteen (from my home in Georgia) allegedly to attend college but really to apply myself to the eighteen-inch brown trout in the Madison River and to meander mapless along the Bridger Range atop cross-country skis. Just before Thanksgiving, I put my name on a hitchhikers' bulletin board in Bozeman and that's when the Laundromat guy called. He was headed to Denver, where my uncle was expecting me. But there was a catch: The driver had to make stops all along the way to tinker with coin-operated washing machines and dryers. And, oh yes, his truck's heater wasn't working properly.

I was in no position to quibble, so for twenty-four hours beginning at 6:00 A.M. Thanksgiving eve we rode side by side through some of the most beautiful country on God's earth: mountain peaks shaped like knife blades along Montana's Paradise Valley, soft foothills belonging to the Bighorn Range framing a Crow Indian Reservation on the Wyoming border, and great golden waves of grassland rolling eastward, forever, from Fort Collins, Colorado.

But what I remember most about that trip, besides the blinding snow that made all the above tragically impossible to see, were the Laundromats: Mack's Cowboy Suds in Livingston, Montana, and The Soap & Save Shop in Sheridan, Wyoming, and May's pan-fried venison burgers off a side grill at the Western Wash-o-rama in Casper. At each stop I huddled against a row of spinning dryers for extra warmth while my repairman companion tinkered in frustration with idle machinery, resorting more than once to a few well-placed kicks from his Texas steel-toe "shit-packer" boots to get washers jump-started.

My looks were in full harmony with my spirits that Thanksgiving sunrise as I finally knocked on my uncle Barry's door with frozen hands and a hunched back. He answered, looked straight at me, and said "Yeesss?" in such a way that I knew I had to hurriedly discard layers of gloves, hats, and clothes before he slammed the door in fright. When I was sufficiently unmasked, I watched Barry throw back his head, bellow, and then give me a smothering bear hug that nearly squeezed all the cold breath right out of me.

I remember that hug vividly. I remember my uncle's skinny, almost bony arms against my back, the feel of his warm, bearded cheek against mine, the shine of his handsomely balding head and gently intense hazel eyes as he finally let go. But what I remember most about that hug was that there were so few others like it over the years that followed. Barry suffered from a severe form of arthritis known as ankylosing spondylitis, and the terrible pain of his condition would gradually make such things as hugs nearly impossible. My own stooped back and curled fingers—the result of a frosty-hard truck seat and cold wrenches jabbing at my sides—would go away with a good cup of coffee and a little sleep. But Barry's condition was permanent. Indeed, it would eventually kill him. But you'd never guess the constant pain he was in from his personality, which was always cheerful. His hips may have needed re-placing and his spine was literally crumbling, but Barry somehow found an inner will to endure, quietly, all that was bad in life in order to enjoy, finally, all that was good: art and music, close friends and good food. And travel. Definitely travel.

Over breakfast, I described in great detail the journey down from Bozeman. Barry laughed, saying it reminded him of adventures from Jack Kerouac's famed novel *On the Road*.

"Jack who?" I said with unabashed teenage ignorance.

Barry frowned at my slothful reading habits and padded off to his bookshelf for an old Penguin paperback version of the novel with mod sixties jacket lettering and well-thumbed pages inside. I devoured the book that same night, with great pleasure. But it didn't become my Bible or turn me into a latter-day, finger-snapping beatnik drifter. To be sure, I thrilled to the mad, coast-to-coast dashes in Dean Moriarty's mud-spattered '49 Hudson and the reefer-enhanced detours through Mexico's Chihuahuan Desert. But my favorite passages involved velocity of a different sort: the blistering bebop jam sessions in Harlem and at Jamson's Nook in San Francisco, where Dean and Sal Paradise sat in beery, shoe-tapping ecstasy, staring at eternity.

What *On the Road* did for me, though, was declare once and for all that it was okay to want to travel ambitiously. Motion was healthy. It didn't make you crazy to stare at maps for hours on end or to want to be a stamp collector—not of the boring postal type but of those inky, unreadable visas pounded into passports by gruff men in uniforms with shoulder belts guarding borders between nations so obscure only Scrabble devotees can spell them.

This was a big truth Barry himself had begun to learn during his own college days in the mid-1960s. The night before a tedious final exam, he and his best friend, John Rauch, decided with admirable irresponsibility to drop out of school and take off for New Orleans in John's black '55 Chevy—without telling anyone. After a day of worry, my grandmother sent my dad looking all over Memphis, Tennessee, for the college fugitives, including to the docks of

3

Lake McKellar, an old oxbow lake of the Mississippi River, where a small wooden boat belonging to Barry and John was found floating empty except for their tattered tennis shoes. Just their shoes.

Before the Memphis police could begin dragging the lake for bodies, Barry called to tell the family he and John had decided to seek their fortunes on the narrow, decadent streets of New Orleans by, well, selling encyclopedias door to door. In four weeks of trying they each sold exactly one set—to poor families on the other side of the Canal Street ferry in a section called Algiers. But the real payoff came at night. After work they'd hop the St. Charles Street trolley for the French Quarter to listen to Dixieland bands all night long at the now-defunct Annex bar right next to Preservation Hall. These sessions were the real deal, unsugared by the tourism crush yet to come, featuring soaring, swinging, brassy bands filled with old black horn players born as far back as the 1800s. At sunrise, hoarse from cigarettes and hours of shouting praise, Barry and John would walk the five blocks to Café du Monde right on the Mississippi River for hot beignets and coffee laced with teaspoons of fresh ground chicory.

The pair returned to Memphis broke, their car running on fumes, with no plans to return to college. Soon afterward they took off for good, this time to the faraway mountains of Denver, which is where, years later, Barry gave me the copy of *On the Road*. I'm not sure where I lost that tattered paperback. I don't remember taking it in my duffel bag to the Congo right out of college as a Peace Corps volunteer. I do remember rereading *somebody's* copy by kerosene lamp in my tiny village house, a mud-walled affair where I'd wake up each morning, build a fire on the dirt floor, boil some water for tea, then open my front door to 2000 B.C.

I continued to travel restlessly in the years that followed—Guatemala, Peru, Kenya, Egypt, the Amazon rain forest. I sent Barry at least one postcard dotted with candle wax from an unheated log cabin in Alberta, Canada. We saw each other now and again at home in our native South—at family re-unions, a wedding, the birth of a new child. Always it was great to be together, especially in the familiar trappings of home, either in Memphis where we were both born or in Atlanta where I grew up. Over hickory-smoked barbecue pork sandwiches slathered with coleslaw right on the bun (the way they do it in Memphis), Barry would ask all about my latest travels. And there, overlooking the Mississippi River, high atop the downtown bluffs of Memphis, I'd go on longer than I probably should have about some odyssey or other. Then Barry would flag the waiter, order another round of Abita beers, and proceed to capture, perfectly, in just a few short words, the sentiment of the moment: "But don't you think—no matter what the trip—that the best part of a journey is coming back home? Don't you think?"

He was absolutely right, of course, though the point had never occurred to me until it was articulated by this same man who, more than anyone, had validated my need to go far, far away.

Barry traveled, too, for work and pleasure, but mostly to countries less physically demanding of travelers: Germany, France, Italy, all over the United States. With each year his arthritis grew worse, his posture more stooped. Inches disappeared from his height. When I saw him now he'd firmly grab my shoulders and bring me into a semi-embrace, forgoing the bear hugs of years past. The doctors told him the vertebrae in his spine, battered by years of inflammation that obliterated cartilage, were literally fusing together. Reduced mobility was matched by increased pain, and Barry began traveling more and more to exotic locations only in his keen imagination.

"Quito," he said to me one night over beers in Washington, D.C. "Quito, Ecuador. Of all the places in the world, that's where I'd like to go before my days are done. Snow-capped volcanoes, panpipe music, people in ponchos, pigtailed Otavaleno Indians selling rugs on the streets. Quito."

That conversation in Washington came during Barry's final years. He was in town for business, and before heading off to a pub on D.C.'s Dupont Circle to catch up, we slipped inside a drugstore so he could pick up some prescription painkillers. That's not what he told me. He just said he had to pick up something. He was severely bow-backed now. He walked bent far forward with his arms swinging well behind his back. In public, people noticed. Some stared. But Barry was so determined not to let his condition defeat him totally that he never discussed his discomfort. Never.

I last saw Barry in 1992 on a bitterly cold February night at my home in Takoma Park, Maryland, just outside Washington. Even a simple, firm handshake at the door, nothing more, brought a wince to his face. Still, nothing could impede the celebration that filled a room when Barry simply took off his coat, gingerly lowered himself into a chair, and started talking about work, life, travel. He'd just had a wonderful trip to the New Mexico desert, he said, where a tumble-down tavern served up a bowl of goat-meat chili so exquisite that God's face seemed to appear momentarily among the jalapeños and Navajo red beans.

In an act of stubborn defiance against the ways of the universe, I decided to grill steaks outside that winter night, racing out in my mittens to flip two-inch-thick T-bones despite the ten-degree temperature that was freezing water pipes up and down my street. For dessert we had big, soul-warming bowls of fresh strawberries picked from some sunny place far, far away.

After dinner, I surprised Barry by pulling out a small, colorful wool rug intricately woven by Andean Indians.

"Where'd you get it?" he asked.

I placed the rug in his hands.

"Quito," I said.

He looked at me in stunned silence.

A magazine assignment two months earlier had taken me to the fabled city of his imagination. "I bought it from pigtailed Otavaleno Indians selling rugs on the street, just like you said they would be," I told him.

Barry drank in every last detail of the trip like a fine wine, slowly and with great groans of pleasure as I talked. He repeatedly declined my offer of the rug as a gift. Instead, he searched my house for the perfect wall from which to hang it. Looking back, I think he knew even then what was about to happen.

We sipped Hennessey cognac and smoked Dominican cigars in my warm den that freezing night until 2:00 A.M. when I put him in a cab for his hotel room, waving good-bye from the sidewalk.

Introduction

◆ ◆ ◆

The surgery, six months later in August, was horrifying in every aspect. Barry lost such an enormous quantity of blood that only massive transfusions of fresh units kept him alive initially.

The objective of attaching a series of stabilizing steel rods along the entire span of his spine required that surgeons enter not from his back but through his abdomen, parting all his major organs to get at the troubled area.

I was busy with work and on the road during the weeks prior to the surgery. Barry and I played phone tag, and I left a final message while passing briefly through the Denver airport.

"Hey, Barry, don't eat the hospital food. I'll send you barbecue from Memphis. Keep your chin up."

Only from others did I learn that Barry had finally restored his long-owned 1964-and-a-half Mustang convertible to mint condition before the operation. He then donned a Panama hat, put the roof down, and drove across Denver to visit friends, essentially saying good-bye.

Barry survived the surgery but developed problems soon afterwards in intensive care. His pulse weakened, his breathing grew shallow. His body temperature began to drop. He was in and out of consciousness for the next three days, unable to talk. Incredibly, he smiled weakly when awake, remaining bravely cheerful through it all, despite the enormous pain.

But battered by a lifetime of physical struggle and prescription medicines, his body finally just gave out. My aunt Diedra was by his side at the end, holding his hand. With Barry's heart just moments from flat-lining, she tried with all her might to call him back, speaking into his ear through the den of beeping machines and physicians giving orders. She searched her mind for the most powerful appeal she could muster and settled, finally, on something desperately basic: his sense of home.

"Not yet, Barry," she cried. "Not now. You've got to take me back to Memphis. You've got to take me home to Graceland first."

For years he had promised to escort her to that peculiar mansion on the outskirts of Memphis which, for better or worse, has become a southern Mecca. Now, in an act of bad manners, he was threatening to leave on a final journey without making good on his promise.

"Graceland, Barry. Graceland."

Somehow, from somewhere, he heard her. His pulse bounced back. His breathing grew stronger. He was still unconscious but he was doing the best he could. And for several minutes he *was* back home, back in this world, holding his wife's hand for a final, brief good-bye before packing up his bags and hitting the road for good. A faraway look of peaceful sleep overcame his face . . . and he was gone.

Nearly a decade has now passed and I think of Barry every day, but especially right before taking that first step of a new trip. There's a good-luck ritual I've adopted over the years of sitting on my backpack or duffel bag or suitcase for a few moments at the start of each journey. I just sit on the luggage. It's an old Russian tradition passed down by my wife's ancestors. And while I sit there I imagine Barry perched right next to me, all packed and ready to go too, ready to offer his protective presence as his duty for first nurturing inside me the travel seed so long ago.

So in all the essays that follow in this collection, Barry is by my side, tagging along. He's never mentioned by name, but he's definitely there, equipped with a strong and capable back as he walks across the island of Sicily, hunts wild pigs with Amazonian Indians, gets marooned on a desert island in the Bahamas, and rides horses along Central Asia's ancient Silk Road.

I like to think, too, that there is a strong sense of home in these travel essays. That is, wherever I go I try to get at what's most important and intimate about a place, to find out what things large or small make it unique, make a place *home,* for the people who live there. It's my goal to get invited inside a culture's front door, to make friends whenever possible, to avoid simply passing through, never daring to knock. Entrée on these pages comes in surprising ways—during a street-side haircut in Hanoi, Vietnam, or while unexpectedly leading a parade through a Bavarian village or while spending Christmas Eve alone with a poor innkeeper's family in the Colombian Andes.

But regardless of the destination, each of these stories traveled back in my pocket to be penned, finally, at my own home, a place I love best, a house filled with century-old wood floors and the smell of spelt-flour cookies from my wife Catherine's famously never-the-same-twice recipe. My son, Sasha, gambols across those floors on noisy, three-year-old bare feet waiting impatiently for the cookies to cool while, upstairs, I work at my writing table. And within easy view of where I sit there hangs a wool rug woven by pigtailed Indians on the high mountain streets of Quito, Ecuador. My atlas reminds me that at more than nine thousand feet, Quito is one of the highest cities I've ever been to in all my travels. Which is to say it's way up there near heaven. Which is why, by now, I'm sure Barry's been there.

1
Around the World

1

Hanoi Haircut

Against a worn strip of water buffalo leather, the Vietnamese barber slapped his straight razor back and forth. He paused to tilt my head back, leaving my Adam's apple fully exposed to the blade. Looking up now, I saw the flowers of a flaming mimosa tree, its branches forming the delicate ceiling of this one-man outdoor barber shop. I smelled the incense of a nine-hundred-year-old Confucian temple located around one hundred feet away. I heard the bright bells of bicycles gliding down a wide Hanoi boulevard.

Yet we'd gotten off to a bad start, this barber and I. I figured he was trying to fleece me when, after I asked how much he charged, he demurred. But he was just being polite in Vietnamese fashion, saying I would pay afterward, as much as I wanted, only if I was happy. When I pressed the issue, he just waved me into his wooden chair. I got in, huffing, our cultures colliding as we attempted to communicate.

"How many fallen yellow leaves do you have?" the barber asked me, still whacking his long, gleaming razor against the leather strop. He was asking

13

my age. "Thirty-three fallen yellow leaves," I said. He asked what country I was from. "America," I said. "I killed many Americans during the war," he said. "Many Americans." Moments later, I felt the razor on my throat.

It's a fact of traveling life that if you wander far enough from home, sooner or later you will need a haircut while on the road. It's an experience I learned early on not to dismiss as routine. With an open mind and flexible fashion standards, the overseas haircut can be one of the most edifying, satisfying experiences the road has to offer.

After all, the barber's chair is where you'll experience the most intimate contact you're likely to have with the local culture. Even the friendliest guides and cabbies and rickshaw drivers don't touch you, don't run their fingers through your hair and fuss over the aesthetic possibilities of your face. When it's over, you're transformed, usually in more ways than one. If nothing else, you'll look more like the locals, because no matter what kind of haircut you ask for, what you get is the local variety. Forget the charms of being invited into people's homes or wearing colorful national clothing: A local haircut is your one best shot at partial assimilation, a chance to assume a part of the local culture on your own body.

My first overseas haircut came in Africa, under the eave of a grass hut in a tiny village in the Democratic Republic of the Congo. When the barber finished cutting, he obsessively swept up every bit of hair from the dirt floor, then plucked, one by one, the tiniest fallen hairs from my neck and shoulders. These he poured posthaste down the hole of a latrine, saying he didn't want any of the nearby witch doctors using my hair to work bad juju on me. Now *there's* a service worth a handsome tip.

Once, in a slum in Bangladesh, an eighteen-year-old barber cut my hair and then massaged my shoulders, temples, hands, and finally—saying it would help me better pray to Allah—my eyelids, rubbing them so gently it nearly put me to sleep. In an oil town deep in the Amazon jungle, I once found the only place for haircuts was the local brothel. A prostitute dutifully trimmed away my sludge-flecked hair, then seemed disappointed when, newly beautified, I didn't avail myself of other services. In Istanbul, amid the tangled alleys lining the Bosphorus, a barber once nearly set me on fire, using a lighted match to give me the sort of "singe trim" around the ears that was the fashion there. It turned out to be the best haircut I've ever had.

That afternoon under the mimosa tree in Vietnam, my education was continuing. The barber had finished shaving my face and was putting away his razor. Only then did it seem safe again to raise the issue of price. Years of travel had led me to anticipate this tactic: The merchant insists on an enormous, unmovable price after the service is rendered. But I hesitated bringing up the subject again. The barber seemed to read my mind nevertheless.

"We Vietnamese people are not so direct as you. We are easier in our ways," he said. "For us, it is not so hard to trust."

He pulled out his scissors now.

"So will I like this haircut?" I asked with a conspicuous hint of sarcasm.

The barber gave me a bright, scolding laugh, his dark eyes narrowing above wrinkles that suggested he had at least sixty fallen yellow leaves himself.

"I, young friend, am a sculptor. Under my hands, rough stone is turned into a beautiful, delicate statue."

"So it's an art form, haircutting?" I asked.

He responded sharply, leaving me temporarily confused. "No, it is not an art form. Few people can really cut hair. It is a *high* art form."

At this he lapsed into ebullient laughter again—and so did I, my suspicions gradually receding.

He began cutting my hair without once asking what I wanted, a common occurrence in my travels in the developing world. Nor did I try to direct him except to ask that he not cut it too short.

"Why do you cut hair outdoors?" I asked. "Is it too expensive to rent a shop?"

He feigned huge offense. "Not at all," he said, now working the scissors across my bangs. "I have many, many clients. I have plenty of money for a shop. But why be a prisoner of walls? I prefer to be outdoors. I feel the wind and sun every day when I work. I smell the flowers of this tree." He then quoted a line from Ho Chi Minh: " 'There's nothing as good as freedom and independence. Nothing.' "

Branches swayed overhead as I glanced at the mirror on the mimosa trunk. My hair was taking shape, reminding me again that, when it comes to barbering, the world is not yet one village. I'd found in most of Latin America that timid cutting tends to leave your hair longer than desired. (The Che influence?) In Central Asia, you're lucky if you have any hair left when it's over. And in Vietnam, you tend to get both: really short hair on the sides and foppishly long hair on top. Staring uncertainly at the mirror, I reasoned that at least while I stayed in Vietnam I would be a work of art.

Since his adolescence, the barber told me, all he'd wanted to do was cut hair. It was his one true passion. Even during the war he cut hair for his platoon. "I was working on someone's hair once when your country sent rockets into our camp. Rockets everywhere. I jumped into a foxhole still holding my scissors and comb."

Now that the war was over, the barber wanted nothing more to do with it. "It was a bad time. I fought to make my country free. Now I just want to do good, to make people beautiful."

As a matter of principle, he said, he never bought any of the tools in Vietnam still widely recycled from old war material. "When I need new scissors, I ask: Was this made from a tank? From a cannon? If so, I don't buy."

My haircut was nearly over now, and the barber suddenly made an announcement. The snipping stopped. "You're the first American whose hair I've cut," he said, swinging around till our eyes met. "I shot at many Americans, but never this. You're my first."

Before I could tell him the honor was mine, he asked a favor. "When you go home, will you thank your president for lifting the economic embargo on my country?"

I said I would, glad of the chance to redeem a little of my initial personal brusqueness toward him.

"Then," he added, a scold returning to his voice, "tell your president to lift the embargo on Cuba."

My haircut was complete. But the barber wasn't finished. It is, I've found, the rare faraway haircut that does not serve up at least one new experience, whether it's the eyelid massage or the finishing spray of lime juice a barber in Mexico once put in my hair. From a leather pouch, the Vietnamese barber pulled out six long, narrow metal tools. They looked like surgical equipment. One tool had a pointed tip. Another had a strange tiny spoon at the end. A pair of tweezers was so long they looked like chopsticks joined at the fat end. "I want to clean your ears," he said.

"Not everyone needs this," he said. "But looking at your ears, I can see you need help. Can you hear okay?"

"I think so," I said.

He assured me he wouldn't hurt me. This was an ancient Vietnamese tradition, but, he added dolefully, one that was dying out. "I tell young people, just like the floors of your house or cups for tea, you have to clean your ears. But no one understands anymore. With skillfully cleaned ears, a man is a new man."

He went to work, guided by a penlight fastened awkwardly to the side of his head. I braced myself. In went the pointed thing. Then the spoon thing. Then the tweezers. After some initial apprehension, the experience became oddly tranquilizing and even enjoyable. It felt like I was getting a massage inside my head.

As he worked, the barber told me he cut fifteen to twenty heads a day, every day, and he never missed work due to illness. Quite a record for a man his age, I thought. What was the secret?

"Never sleep late," he said. "Eat when you're hungry. And always help people. Always love people." Then he added, "I pray, too. I go to the pagoda twice a month and light incense and pray for the peace and happiness of all the people in the world. I never leave anyone out. I've prayed for you all your life."

Shortly thereafter, he pulled his barber's sheet off me as if from a masterpiece. Shave, haircut, ear cleaning. If not a totally new man, I felt like I was refurbished.

"What do I pay you if I'm very, very happy?" I asked, now quite won over by the original gentleman's arrangement.

"Nothing," he said with unbreachable finality. "That you are happy is big enough payment for me."

I protested effusively, of course, even tried leaving the money in the crotch of the tree. But it was no good. "You owe me nothing," he said.

We parted company with a handshake. As I walked away, it struck me that cutting a traveler's hair must be nearly as interesting for the barber as for the traveler. Perhaps I had given him a minor amusement, a new, small way of thinking about himself. He, meanwhile, had given me something much more than a haircut. Thanks to him, I could hear just a little bit better.

Or is the word *listen*?

2

Christmas Miracle
in the Andes

How many nights will you be staying?" the Indian innkeeper asks me, leaning over his dusty desk. He speaks in slow, accented Spanish. Behind him, an assortment of wooden Christmas ornaments festoons the inn's aged door. The stone fireplace is a gentle tempest of logs and cracking flames. It is December 23.

"Three nights," I say, lowering my backpack to the warm stone floor. The innkeeper arches an eyebrow. "So you'll be staying through Christmas?"

"Yes."

"And you're alone?" He glances over my shoulder.

"Yes."

"I see," he says.

I gather my gear and follow the innkeeper, whose name is Guillermo, down a narrow hallway to my room. Through a window, a liquid flaming sun is sinking toward nine-thousand-foot peaks outside this rural mountain village in southern Colombia.

"You're our only guest," Guillermo says, unlocking my room and handing me the key. "There are no other visitors here." I can almost read the rest of his thoughts: "We never get backpackers at Christmastime. Never. And the Colombian tourists—they have all gone home to be with their families, of course, for the holidays."

I settle quickly into my room, then hurry outside to catch the last of the sunset. I pass unlit Christmas candles, thick and red and half-used, scattered throughout the inn.

My being here is no accident. I want to be at this distant spot, far from my own country, a lone traveler, at Christmastime. The holiday in America always leaves me feeling a bit blue. While others relish the crowds, the shopping, the yuletide specials on TV, I'm never quite able to catch the "spirit"—to get festive on cue—when so much of the package seems like a scripted marketing opportunity. The best solution, I decide: Sample the holiday elsewhere. Which is how I wind up among these Andean mountains.

I follow a short path down from the inn to the edge of Lake Guamues, the largest, highest, most beautiful piece of fresh water in Colombia. The indigo surface is cradled by forested mountains turned blond by the waning light. In the cool alpine air, I pass ponchoed Indians in bowler hats. A young boy with braided hair carries a panpipe as he herds llamas along the shore. The lake is shaped like a giant teardrop.

I take a seat and watch as a series of final, awesome sunbeams falls to earth. The myth runs that a powerful medicine man created this lake and these mountains from the bodies of a feuding husband and wife—and the result is absolute peace for all who live here. I can feel it. A stillness spreads through my road-weary body. Nearby, a peasant farmer is harvesting potatoes from the black earth and humming a familiar tune. I listen. I recognize the song. "Noche de Paz." Silent night.

Christmas Miracle in the Andes

The last of the sun disappears. The panpipe in the distance begins to play, flutelike and joyful, getting farther and farther away. In a manner of speaking, Christmas this year, for the first time in my life, may very well be a religious experience.

The best Christmas holidays I've ever spent were overseas in obscure corners of the world—in Africa, Central Asia, South America. There was that Christmas in the Congo, for instance, sitting down to goat meat and *fufu* with other bearded, ponytailed Peace Corps volunteers under a rustling palm tree. There was that time, too, in faraway Kyrgyzstan, gathering juniper branches in the snow for window decorations and exchanging used books wrapped in boxer shorts.

At such far-flung venues the holiday ritual is simpler: You call to your table whatever American expats happen to be within easy travel distance. There's no media bombardment telling you to buy, buy, buy, so you don't. There's nothing to purchase anyway. You just come together for a daylong meal with a little too much wine tossed in. Just like Thanksgiving. It's love unhindered by the distractions of list-making and gift-wrapping, fellowship without credit card heroics.

And so it was a few years ago I found myself alone in South America at the end of a long writing trip. Christmas was just a few days away. I could have flown home in time, but I had already missed the two-month, hyperventilating buildup to Christmas back in the States. Arriving now, with the holiday peaking, might give me the Christmas equivalent of the bends. I'd be coming up way too fast. So I drifted into the mountains of Colombia instead.

If overseas travel is a way of forgetting your own culture while experiencing another, then Christmas, by my tastes, is a perfect time to travel. I opened a map of Colombia and picked the tiny, isolated village of El Encano on Lake Guamues (also known as Laguna de la Cocha), three hundred miles southwest of Bogota. I decided that whatever Christmas was at this little place, that's what Christmas would be for me, too. There'd be no handful of American expats around this time, either. Just me and whatever I found. Just me and . . . Christmas.

I awake the morning before Christmas to the sound of cows being milked outside my room. From my bed, I peek outdoors through a badly cracked window at Guillermo. He's sitting in the distance on a stool, humming, milking a cow—*squish, squish*—into a tin bucket. An explosion of morning sunlight shows that he's wearing the same clothes he had on the night before—old canvas pants and a llama-wool sweater. These are the only clothes he'll wear during my entire stay. The cracked window has been repaired with a cheap opaque tape.

But the place has perks. I exit my room and Guillermo hands me a steaming cup of just-made Colombian coffee. He's added cream straight from the cow and the result is sublime. "Come see all the hummingbirds," he says brightly as I moan with every sip.

Outside, the weather has warmed quickly to a dreamlike morning of shirtsleeve sunshine. The lake below us is a giant, blue-white mirage of reflected light. Most striking, though, are the flowers. They grow wild. They grow everywhere. Orchids, asters, daisies. They climb along the stone walls of the inn and up toward the Spanish tile roof, offering their nectar to two dozen red and green hummingbirds.

"December is the start of our best weather," Guillermo says. "It's our springtime."

I take another sip of coffee, standing in the sunshine, and wonder what blustery winter weather is making mischief back home in Washington, D.C.

The inn grounds double as a family farm, and just then Guillermo's three children arrive carrying eggs and more milk from a barn out back. They are Gemri, a boy, eight; Guillermo Jr., seventeen; and Dorys, twenty-two. Guillermo himself is fifty, but looks younger, with a thick mane of black hair sans a single gray strand.

Guillermo is fretting now, his face lined with perplexity. He doesn't quite know what to make of me. I tell him I'm going for a long walk along the lake. But before I leave, he tells me again that I'm the inn's only guest. In fact, he says, there's never been a guest at Christmastime in the twenty-five-year history of this out-of-the-way establishment.

"Hmmm," I say. "Okay. See you this afternoon."

For hours, I wander along grassy bluffs overlooking the lake. I see more llamas and shepherds—and cows with snow-white herons perched gently atop their backs. I see a tiny island in the distance with a shrine to the region's adopted saint, Nuestra Señora de Lourdes. She watches over local fishermen who in turn honor her each year with a huge feast of stewed guinea pig, an Andean delicacy.

It's nearly dark and the air is again chilly by the time I return to the inn. Guillermo has built another fire and has lit all the candles for Christmas Eve. My boots and socks are wet from my hike, so I place them by the fire to dry. I join Guillermo on a long bench pulled up close, and thaw myself in the warmth of the flames. But seeing my socks hanging down from the mantel, I feel a stab of homesickness for the first and last time during this trip. I can't hide the feeling as I describe for Guillermo the tradition of stockings turned magically full by Santa Claus on Christmas Eve.

No such stocking tradition exists in Colombia, he says. Then he gives me a long, vaguely fatherly look. "Why are you not home now?" he says. "Home with people you know? Then you could have this tradition."

The tinge of sadness in his eyes leaves me touched. I rush to tell him my philosophical beliefs aren't quite in harmony with the holiday back home. I'm very, very happy to be here, I say. He accepts this readily with a look of kind respect.

"My family, we are Catholics," Guillermo says, "so Christmas is very special to us. We also have this man Santa Claus in Colombia, but he does not come to our home."

Now I'm the one feeling a tinge of sadness. "Why not?" I ask.

"Many years ago, when the children were very small, we stopped giving gifts in our family. We are a poor country. Even me, with the inn and the farm, I am a poor man. So the children know about Santa Claus, but they don't believe in him because he never comes to visit their home."

I say nothing, trying to show him the same respect he'd shown me earlier. His voice trails off into the fireplace flames.

It's past dinnertime now, and I hear sounds of cooking in a back-room kitchen.

"Could I order some dinner?" I ask. This strikes Guillermo as funny somehow. "There's nothing to order," he says, laughing heartily now. "There's no menu! You're a guest of my family tonight, not of the inn."

It has grown completely dark outside, and I slip out to view the Andean night sky. Christmas Eve has arrived in full, heralded by a billion bright stars. Only the sumptuous odor of good cooking inside finally lures me back.

At nine o'clock, at a table set up by the fireplace, we sit down to eat. Guillermo's daughter, Dorys, has been doing all the cooking. I still have not seen Guillermo's wife, and there's no place set for her now. I sense a sad story behind this somehow, and I decide not to ask.

I survey the table and am incredulous. Dorys and Guillermo Jr. have covered each plate with a thick bed of yellow rice crowned by a large, roasted chicken breast. The breast is stuffed with minced liver and covered with a sticky sweet sauce. It is a fantastic feast by this family's meager means, and I consider the thought that I've never been offered a more valuable gift.

Guillermo says a short prayer, and we begin eating. The chicken is wondrous, and the accompanying red wine is quite decent. Dessert is a bowl of very sweet white-bean soup eaten only at Christmastime in Colombia. When I compliment Dorys on her cooking, she shrugs modestly. "These are recipes our mother taught me many years ago." There's an air of despondency in her expression that again keeps me from asking more. Guillermo, clearly, is raising these children alone.

The children ask me various questions about America throughout dinner. At one point, eight-year-old Gemri says, "Tell us a Christmas story from your country."

I decide to steer clear of the Rudolph and Grinch stories, both of which end with children happily receiving mountains of gifts. In the candlelight of that table, I tell instead a simple story of a Christmas Eve when I was a child in Georgia and times were hard for my family. My father was out of work, except for a low-paying job delivering newspapers. I helped him with his work on Christmas Eve morning so he could come home quickly. My mom and sister made hot chocolate for us when we returned and we spent the rest of the day arranging strings of popcorn across our Christmas tree. We all wanted very badly for it to snow that evening, even though it rarely snowed where we lived. But that night it happened—there were snow flurries. The first time ever on Christmas Eve!

"Un milagro," Gemri says. "A miracle. They happen at Christmas if you really want them to. Papa says so."

"No," Guillermo says quickly. "I said a miracle happened to me *one time* at Christmas when I wished for it."

I look at Guillermo quizzically. "Come," he says, standing. "The children know this story. I will tell you outside while they clear the table."

We step out into the sparkling night air, and the stars are even more lustrous than before. Whole galaxies are visible, cloudlike and full of mystery. Guillermo and I walk toward the lake, happily full of food and wine, while he talks.

"I tell you this story because without it, you would have no place to stay tonight," he begins. "Twenty-five years ago I had nothing. No money. No job. In these mountains, it's hard to find work. My dream was humble: to have a little farm and a place for travelers to stay.

"Then God helped me. It was Christmas Eve, twenty-five years ago—a starry night like this. We were visiting my wife's family, who are city people. Her brother was very, very drunk that night and he asked me to help him walk home. I was upset by this, but he really needed my help. He staggered and swayed so much. One time he almost fell down on the sidewalk and I rushed to catch him and that's when I saw it. On the ground, in the dark, was a little yellow bundle. I reached down and picked it up, not knowing what it was. Then I saw it was money. Lots of money. Ten thousand pesos [\$600]! I had never held so much money in my hand in my whole life.

"I was shocked. I looked around to see if anyone was looking for it, but I saw no one. It was so much money. For three days I watched this spot from a distance, waiting to see someone looking for it so I could give it back. But no one came."

Guillermo and I have turned around in our walk and are nearing the inn again. The front windows bear the faint glow of dying fireplace embers. The children have already gone to sleep.

"With that money," Guillermo says, "I bought my first cow. And I bought the materials to build this inn. All of it came from a sidewalk, this money. *A sidewalk.*"

We step through the front door and feel the warmth inside. "That," Guillermo says, "is my miracle."

The story has left me bewitched, my mind in a happy spin. But now it is time for bed inside this giant Christmas wonder of an inn.

"Sleep well, Señor Mike," Guillermo says. "We will speak more tomorrow."

"*Feliz Navidad,* Señor Guillermo."

The next day I rise late, wondering if the events of the night before were a dream, a fairy tale. But Guillermo and family are still here. It's Christmas morning, and they are soon giving me coffee and a sweet, fried corn bread called *bunuelo.*

Later, Guillermo tunes his transistor radio to a Catholic Mass being broadcast out of Bogota, and the family gathers round. There is no Christmas tree here and no evidence whatsoever of gifts having been exchanged. Nor is there any palpable letdown hovering in the air, that Christmas ether of dashed expectations common in affluent countries after the inevitable dissatisfaction with things.

The day is a leisurely one, and I spend it all with the family. Guillermo Jr. and I chop wood for the evening fire. Guillermo Sr. helps Gemri with his homework. Dorys cooks another handsome meal. The family is happy to-day—and very, very wealthy. Less really is more. Stripped to its core, Christmas is slower, deeper, bigger. I feel fully present for the holiday for the first time in years.

But I can't shake the impulse: I want to give the family a gift. My cultural background leaves me feeling incomplete unless I wrap something up and hand it over. I've never spent a Christmas in my entire life, I realize, without giving at least one small thing to *somebody*.

But I have nothing except what's in my wallet. I'm traveling light—and nothing's for sale around the lake on Christmas Day. The next morning, Guillermo hands me a bill for three nights' stay totaling all of $18. None of the food has been included. I hand him the equivalent of $30, intending that he take it all, but he promptly returns $12.

"Please, Guillermo," I say. "It's a Christmas gift. This is a tradition in my country."

"But you have come here to escape your traditions," he says.

Before I can protest, he continues. "You have noticed that my wife does not live with us. She had to take a distant job in another village to help earn money for the family. She could not come home for Christmas this year. You, too, are away from your home, and we have taken care of you. Maybe that means people where she is are taking care of her."

I nod that I understand just as the children step forward to say good-bye. It's strange, but I feel as if I've known this family for many years now. They've taken an ancient celebration and made it new for me by, ironically, omitting everything new and modern and so making the holiday recognizable again.

I lift my backpack to my shoulders, ready to leave.

"We weren't expecting you," Guillermo says. "Don't you see? You were our miracle this year. You came at Christmastime. You somehow found us. There's nothing left for you to give us or us to give you. It was a nice holiday that way. Don't you think?"

3
Sibling Revelry on the Rhine

I have no way to prove it, but I may be the only American eighteen-year-old ever to be honorary grand marshal of a major parade through the streets of a German city. Dressed improbably in T-shirt and shamefully old Levi's, my backpack tossed aside, I chanced to lead a multitude of marching, clapping, dancing Rhinelanders in the biggest celebration of their calendar year. And all because years before I was born, Dwight D. Eisenhower came up with a novel idea: Cities could be sisters.

Growing up in small and drowsy Marietta, Georgia, I had heard snatches of lore about how my town had struck sororal union with Linz, Germany, a village of farmers and shopkeepers on the Rhine fifteen or so miles south of Bonn. During World War II, a nineteen-year-old Marietta GI marched into Linz and fell passionately in love with a winsome young damsel there. The two married, and in 1967 their hometowns officially became "sister cities," joining a popular international program now almost fifty years old.

In 1980, when I decided to cast off for Europe before casting my lot with higher education, I put Linz on my itinerary. Marietta city officials cautioned me not to expect too much, but said if I went to the Linz city hall I'd surely get a handshake and friendly directions. Looking at my map of Europe and the eight countries I planned to visit without knowing a single soul, it was calming to know I'd have faint connections at at least one stop.

Sister Cities International—headquartered in Alexandria, Virginia—was founded by Eisenhower in 1956 to let "the people themselves give expression to their common desire for friendship, good will, and cooperation for a better world." That sounded okay to me. Today, more than nine hundred U.S. cities are linked to more than 1,400 foreign municipalities: Washington is sister to Bangkok, Thailand; Los Angeles to Athens, Greece; Lawrence, Kansas, to Hiratsuka, Japan. City-to-city contacts include everything from formal student and cultural exchanges to summits between governing officials. But probably the least publicized and most rewarding way to visit a sister city is simply to do what I did: show up and see what happens.

I scheduled my visit to Linz toward the end of my European trip. This proved to be a stroke of compensatory good luck because the preceding four weeks on the continent were unambiguously problematic.

Headaches began in France, where my hometown buddy Matt and I began our voyage. After an insufferably hot train ride from Paris to Nice, we arrived to find that Matt's backpack had been pilfered from a holding rack. Devastated, all his possessions gone, Matt contemplated an early flight home. But walking the streets of Nice that night, we chanced to spy a young man in a cafe wearing a Wheeler High School letter jacket. Our high school. Matt's jacket. A street cop helped apprehend the man, and five minutes later we were in a dark and squalid alley where all of Matt's possessions lay amid the winnings of five craps shooters.

Miraculously, everything was retrieved. Or almost everything. We were already in Italy when a sexy-sounding Nice police secretary phoned long-distance to Matt's confused parents. "Zee pants. I have zee pants of Matt. He's here one night and leaves zem. Please tell him I have zee pants." Our fathers giggled and our mothers fussed and no one believed our explications upon our return.

Our trip never fully recovered from this early setback. In Greece, despite our assiduous reliance on cheap accommodations, money ran low, prompting a few nights on the beach. This was fine until a pack of five oversized dogs piled on top of us, deciding they too preferred the soft sleeping comfort of down bags. Neither Matt nor I knew the Greek words for "get your own," so the dogs stayed.

Then came the Attack of the Killer Canal Mosquitoes in Venice and the train breakdown in Switzerland. By the time we got to Austria, where Matt and I struck out in different directions, Linz had grown to a minor obsession in my mind. I kept saying the words over and over again in my head: "sister city." A place where I would be welcome without qualifications, where all I had to do was say, "I'm from Marietta," and people would like me. An ersatz hometown.

As my train approached Linz, hugging the soft bends of the Rhine north of Koblenz, I dug from my pack a clean T-shirt and smoothed out the worst wrinkles on my jeans. Minutes later, I was walking up cobblestone streets toward the Linz city hall, noting the ambitious street decorations—bunting along buildings, flower bouquets along narrow streets, banners in German—and that a great many people were dressed in traditional Rhineland clothing.

Reaching city hall, an eighteenth-century building of stucco and wood beams, I found a secretary talking busily on a phone and several people waiting at a counter. I must have presented quite a sight—pack sagging, tin cups jangling, a cast of confused foreignness on my face—because the others waiting gave me a wide berth.

I sidled up to the counter. The secretary put her hand over the phone and said something in rapid, impatient German. "I don't speak German," I answered apologetically. "I'm just a visitor. I'm from Marietta, Georgia. America. I've just come to say hel—"

"Marieettal?" she said.

"Yes, I—"

"You live in that town place?"

"Yes."

"Ach! Gott, oh, Gott!"

She dispatched her phone mate with a slam and approached the counter to shake my hand. Before she reached me, I felt pats on my shoulders as those waiting around me said, "Oh, welcome. Welcome to Linz."

The secretary's name was Christa. "You should have called beforehand," she said, scolding me cheerfully. "The *burgermeister* must see you at once." Behind her I saw incoming phone lines lighting up and blinking. City business was grinding to a halt with my arrival.

Christa waved her hand and two city workers relieved me of my pack and disappeared. Christa dispelled my frown of concern with a luminous smile, and I realized I was watching the opening moves of a hospitality play. The friendship was immediate and unquestioned, the sort I've since heard spoken of by American travelers to sister cities the world over. I hadn't even divulged my name yet and a host of people were busying themselves with my comfort.

"Marieettal," Christa kept saying. "From Marieettal." Apparently there had been no visitors from my town in six months. "The burgermeister will be so surprised and happy to see you. And on such a special day too!"

Before I could ask what she meant Christa ushered me into the burgermeister's office, explaining who I was. I gave my name at last and extended my hand. The burgermeister took it with both of his. He was a short, puffy, excitable man whose limited English was offset by a rich vocabulary of gestures and facial expressions.

"Yes, yes, welcome. Such a pleasure. I go to your city maybe next year. Very beautiful, I hear. Our sister. Welcome . . . and you come today at a good time. There is a *feier* here today. Very big."

"The feier is a celebration, a parade," Christa said. She explained that on this day each summer Linz was the starting point of a major trans-European cycling race. People came from all over the world. The parade would begin at noon, preceding the race. It was 10:00 A.M. now.

"You are such a special guest," the burgermeister said, "I think you should be leader, very biggest leader of the feier."

"You mean grand marshal?" I said. I reflected on how just two months earlier I had been serving high school detention for tardiness to homeroom. But the probability of a background check seemed quite slim to me.

"I accept," I said.

The burgermeister phoned the chairman of the parade committee with the good news; I, meanwhile, inspected a glass case in the office filled with mementos from my hometown: plaques of friendship and cooperation from the Marietta Chamber of Commerce and a delicate model of a C-5A transport plane manufactured there. The items highlighted the role of trade promotion within the sister-city format. Not surprisingly, few U.S. cities big or small have to be told twice: Friends abroad mean friends in business. In Eastern Europe and the former Soviet Union especially, cities now are using sister-city economic contacts to help jump-start moribund economies.

Christa was talking to me. As parade marshal, she said, I now had certain public responsibilities. I took this to mean I needed to comb my hair and tuck in my T-shirt, which I did. At 11:00 A.M. sharp we left for a large banquet room where the burgermeister was to give a speech. The room was filled with about one hundred dignitaries from throughout Europe. Through tall windows I could see a crowd gathering in the town plaza.

Soon I found myself at a front table seated, to my astonishment, between the head of the German Bundestag and the Swedish ambassador to West Germany. As grand marshal, I tried to soak up their attention with convincing grace, fielding questions on U.S. presidential politics while simultaneously beating back memories of sleeping on Greek beaches just weeks before. When the talk of politics turned too serious, I sensed the moment had arrived for me to promote world peace and understanding per the sister-city charter, so I switched the topic of conversation to World Cup soccer.

After a series of toasts by the burgermeister, we all filtered outside into the sunlit square, where several thousand eager people and hundreds of helmeted cyclists now stood. I was shepherded onto a podium with the burgermeister, who wished the cyclists a safe voyage. Then came the word "Marieeetta" over the public-address system, ringing out like an exclamation point. Christa nudged me, "Bow, wave, do something. Here is your introduction." I bowed slightly to the people of Linz. They cheered.

Just then a traditional five-piece band struck up a song, with the statutory tuba grumping "boo-bump-bump, boo-bump-bump." The burgermeister and I filed in behind the band. A nearby clock tower marked noon. The parade had begun.

In our wake followed the other VIPs, a group of schoolchildren in costumes, and the cyclists. The race would officially begin at the Rhine, several blocks away. We took a slow, circuitous route to the river, zigzagging through narrow streets awash with spectators and colorful bunting. In strict deference to parade pecking order, the burgermeister insisted I walk alone at the very head, just behind the band. I summoned TV images of popes and astronauts in such positions and parodied their style, smiling and waving left-right, left-right. After a few blocks, I expanded my repertoire, hamming it up, blowing kisses to babies.

Behind me, the burgermeister kept seeing people in the crowd and pointing down at my head, saying, "Marieeetta! Marieeetta!" All the while, the sense that I was living a World War II victory newsreel was reinforced by the shower of flowers. From second- and third-story windows—shutters flung open—women in aprons threw carnations; others waved scarves and handkerchiefs.

Too soon, we reached the Rhine, where the burgermeister fired a pistol sending the cyclists on their sweaty way. The band boo-bump-bumped a final time and the crowd dissipated. Christa congratulated me.

We retraced our steps along petal-strewn streets to a pub where I was guest of the burgermeister, Christa, and others. Cakes and sausages were the fare, chased down by long drafts of dark beer. I asked the burgermeister about the story of the Marietta GI marrying a woman from Linz. Was it true? He looked at me. "Yes, it's true. That GI is my brother-in-law. He married my sister. They still visit every year. We're family."

Later, picking the last of the petals from my hair, I had to fight off the greedy feeling that I owned this little village, that a key had been given to me and the entire place was mine for the taking. The truer picture, though, the one I really felt, was that I had been handed a gift, one I was supposed to share. The message from Linz was, "This is who we are. This is one part of what we do. And because you are from Marietta and because your village is surely similar to ours in its own way, we invite you in and make you our highest guest and bid you to share our world with yours so that we may be friends always."

My visit to Linz drew to a close with a final frothy beer. The burgermeister was profoundly saddened when I announced I couldn't stay the night. He had already prepared his guest room for me. But he was gracious in bidding me farewell and a quick return.

There remained a certain detail. "My backpack," I said.

He smiled and said, "Oh, it's taken care of."

Chauffeured to the train station in a city vehicle, the streets of Linz receding behind me, I stayed in suspense until the car's trunk was opened, revealing all my gear intact. Minutes later, the 4:05 to Bonn was trundling gently along the Rhine when, searching for something else, I dipped into my pack and discovered the hidden parting gift: a half-dozen sandwiches, a wedge of cheese, and a bottle of wine.

4
A Journey to the End of the Earth ... Really!

et ready to jump, mate! Hurry! Get ready!" My Australian guide, Andrew the lobster diver, is yelling at me. His voice reaches me above the slap of waves breaking against a giant granite rock in the lower Indian Ocean. I cling to the bow of Andrew's beat-up ten-foot dinghy and brace myself for the leap onto the edge of this same rock. Above me, a colony of eight long-whiskered fur seals stares down with perplexed amusement.

Andrew guns the outboard motor and we begin an approach that puts us on an apparent collision course with the stony outcropping. "Here we go!" he yells. "Here we go!"

I've traveled a long, long way to put myself in this precarious position. I've been traveling almost nonstop, in fact, for seventy-two straight hours from the Washington, D.C., area, stopping only to sleep. I've covered 12,018 miles, crossed twelve time zones and lost a whole Saturday to the international date line. I've traveled by plane, bus, taxi, rental car, fishing boat, and now dinghy. I've traveled so far that I've run out of land. I've gone as far as I can go, which was precisely my goal: to travel as close as possible to the exact other side of the planet from the place I call home: Washington, D.C. Cartographers know this as the antipode—pronounced *an*-teh-pode—the global opposite of any given place. Provided I can get up on this slippery, steep-sided, barnacle-encrusted, seal-inhabited rock, I will have put myself as close to Washington's antipode as I possibly can.

If you dig a hole straight down from the U.S. Capitol building, you don't hit China. You hit a speck of water in the lower Indian Ocean. And this rock before me now, Cumberland Rock, just off the extreme southwestern tip of Australia, a rock named after a nineteenth-century ship that sank on a connecting reef, is certifiably the nearest land mass to D.C.'s antipode. You can't get closer and still have solid ground under your feet.

If you're a burned-out Washington bureaucrat and you really, *really*, *really*, *REALLY* want to get away from beeping faxes and Lewinsky blather, this is where you come: Cumberland Rock, Australia. The end of Earth. It's one hundred feet long, fifty feet wide and extends maybe thirty feet above sea level.

But the hard part, I'm discovering, is actually getting onto the rock. The surrounding seas are famously tricky, littered with the corpses of dozens of sunken ships. Minding your timing, you must carefully ride a swell up to the edge of Cumberland Rock and then, in a split second, jump from your dinghy just before it begins a sliding descent back down the same swell, away from you. Andrew has somehow convinced me that I can do this, perhaps even without injury. And now it's almost time. "Steady, mate. Steady!" he yells above the surging water. "We're getting closer."

It's one last improbable step in a strange trip to a strange place. After the Mother of All Jet Lags, after the endless blur of miles, I'm finally here with a lobster diver as a guide on the underbelly of the globe with this huge chunk of granite just feet before me, getting closer. And closer.

"Now!" Andrew calls. "Now! Jump!" I brace myself and fling my body from the bow of the dinghy, a prayer on my lips.

What self-respecting armchair traveler stuck too long in home port with a dyspeptic boss and absently spinning a globe, hasn't done the mental 180, imagining jamming a pencil through the globe and drifting off to wherever that pencil comes out, far, far away? It's the remote spot we all imagine where no one can possibly find us. We're too far gone.

My own antipode fantasy has always involved a warm tropical atoll where the women wear coconut bras and everyone eats conch steaks grilled over driftwood fires at sunset. So when a slightly daft editor at the *Washington Post* decided that the antipode of D.C. needed to be pinpointed and visited in the name journalistic truth, I was all for it. The place might not live up to my fantasies, but I understood my geography well enough to know that it was summertime down there—wherever it was—because winter weather had set in up here. That was enough to get me going.

But first, of course, if you're going to find Washington's opposite, you have to figure out where Washington itself is. I chose the Capitol dome as my precise starting point, then called the National Geodetic Survey in nearby Silver Spring, Maryland, a federal agency whose raison d'être is admirably unambiguous: location, location, location. NGS can readily give you the latitude and longitude of more than half a million places and features around the United States. In fact, David R. Doyle, senior geodesist at NGS, signs all his E-mails with his name, phone number, and the exact latitude and longitude of his suburban office building (latitude 38–59–33 north, longitude 77–01–50 west).

As it happens, Doyle and a colleague clambered up to the very top of the Capitol dome in 1993 when the Statue of Freedom was brought down for renovation. There, with the aid of more than ten different satellites, the geodesists took an ultraprecise reading of the Capitol's position on the planet, accurate to within five centimeters. Good enough for me, I say. The numbers are

38 degrees 53 minutes 23.31643 seconds north latitude
77 degrees 00 minutes 32.61537 seconds west longitude

Using this data, Doyle then gave me the Capitol's antipodal position, calculated "through the Earth-mass center" using the North American Datum of 1983. The numbers are

38 degrees 53 minutes 23.31643 seconds south latitude
102 degrees, 59 minutes, 27.38463 seconds east longitude

So I had my spot. But I was soon deflated to learn the antipode—12,507 miles away—was in the middle of a big watery nowhere, way down in the lower Indian Ocean near a giant rend in the ocean floor called the Diamantina Fracture, 741.6 miles southwest of Australia. The sea here is seriously deep—15,912 feet, enough to fog anyone's face mask. Only a few wayward trawlers ply the area, seeking hapuka fish. The surrounding waters are known as some of the stormiest and loneliest anywhere in the world.

Why lonely? Because there's absolutely no land in the immediate neighborhood—no islands, no reefs, no rocks, no coconut bras, no grilled conch. Just water. Not exactly fantasy material. It's just as well that I didn't have the two months necessary to drift out to the spot on a trawler.

So I began the hunt for the closest landfall to the antipode, a mission far too exacting for my local library atlas, I decided. I wanted precision. I didn't care how small it was or where it was—an Antarctic cape, a raft of petrified lava, whatever—if it was above sea level and it could support my weight, I wanted to go there.

So I did the only reasonable thing a man in my advanced state of agitation could do: I called the Central Intelligence Agency. I figured it had the best maps in the world. Heck, it probably had spies down near the Diamantina Fracture somewhere. But the post–Cold War CIA gave me a big blunt no-comment on what was clearly an innocent quest made in the name of citizen education and global understanding. What's the CIA hiding, anyway? I wondered. Is there a nuclear-war escape hatch from the Capitol dome straight down to the Fracture? Will members of congress eat hapuka once they get there?

But one mystery at a time. At the moment I was still adrift, cartographically speaking, looking for the nearest landfall to D.C.'s antipode. A friend suggested I call the State Department's Office of the Geographer. There a young and earnest aide named Leo Dillon consulted the department's maps and faxed me what he asserted were the winner and first runner-up of my grand search. The winner, he wrote—and I was skeptical about this from the start—was Cape Leeuwin, Australia, on the southwestern tip of the continent. The runner-up was the tiny French island of St. Paul, 1,368.4 miles west of the antipode in the middle-southern Indian Ocean.

The mention of St. Paul intrigued me. I checked my own atlas. The island was clearly farther away from D.C.'s antipode than the Australian mainland, but it was, it turned out, the closest *island* of any substantial size to the antipode. This restoked my simmering island fantasy enough to make me call the French embassy in Washington for more details. Gary Dwor-frecaut, the embassy archivist, said the island was part of France's Southern and Antarctic Territories. It was extremely windy, had a moderate climate, and a population of eight people.

Then Dwor-frecaut asked me a question: "Why is everyone suddenly interested in St. Paul Island, anyway? It's so obscure."

"Huh?" I said.

He explained that a couple of years back a downtown Washington attorney had called him and, like me, asked lots of questions about little St. Paul. The attorney's intention, apparently, was to quit his job, travel to the island farthest away from Pennsylvania Avenue, and actually live there.

I was stunned. Someone had actually done it. Fevered minds clearly think alike. Dwor-frecaut said he never got the lawyer's name and never heard from him again. Maybe he was one of the eight residents who now called the island home. I wanted to go find this starched-collar Crusoe, of course, but my own antipode quest didn't allow for such an elaborate detour. Consequently, I'm now doomed forever to imagine this guy eating *my* conch steaks over *my* driftwood fires, soiling *my* mythical paradise. Worst of all, he's an *attorney*.

But I digress. Back to the real search. Increasingly, clues were pointing toward southwestern Australia as the closest landfall to D.C.'s antipode. But I had trouble believing the actual spot would be part of the mainland. Surely there was some fragment of land or exposed reef or something offshore. I asked Dillon at the State Department if maybe his maps were missing something. "Maybe," he said. "But it'd have to be really small. The people who would know for sure are at NIMA. You should call NIMA."

The National Imagery and Mapping Agency. Finally, I was in the right hands. This federal agency, located in Fairfax, Virginia, employs arguably the best mapmakers and map readers in the world. NIMA is *the* mapmaking arm of the U.S. military.

"They can't fight without us" is NIMA's informal motto. Even the CIA takes a backseat to NIMA in the map department. Civil and commercial aviators and mariners around the world routinely use NIMA maps and charts, either directly or indirectly, to navigate the planet.

I contacted Jim Ayres, NIMA's scientific advisor for hydrography, and described my problem. He gathered the most relevant and detailed maps in existence, including one borrowed from the Australian military, and went to work. A few days later I got a call.

"Cumberland Rock," Ayres said. "Cumberland Rock, Australia. That's where you've got to go." He'd done a careful search, he assured me, "swinging an arc" from the antipode until, just northwest of Cape Leeuwin, Australia—two miles out to sea—the arc touched an obscure dark speck labeled "rock" on his maps. No other piece of land of any kind in any direction was as close. It was exactly 1,190,811 meters—about 740 miles—east-northeast of Washington's antipode.

I asked Jim again if he was sure about his calculations. "Yes," he said. "But there's something you should probably know." He paused. "This spot looks a little dangerous. It's surrounded by lots of submerged reefs and other perils. It might be a very hard place to get to."

On my end of the phone, I blinked.

Then, almost apologetically, Ayres said, "I hope you have a successful trip."

It takes forever to fly to the other side of the world. The airplane ticket should read "Infinite time required." Just flying from Washington to Los Angeles under normal circumstances is major stuff. But given where I'm headed, the L.A. leg is just the travel equivalent of cracking my knuckles.

After flying five hours to the West Coast, I have a hideous ten-hour layover, spent walking the airport halls looking for celebrities. (Score: Jean-Claude Van Damme.) Just past 9:00 P.M., an hour before my flight to Sydney, there's a special announcement. It's already late for me, past midnight Washington time, so I think I'm dreaming when the P.A. voice says that unusually fierce Pacific headwinds mean the Boeing 747 will need more fuel to cover the enormous distance to Sydney without running dry. A couple of dozen extremely smart passengers agree to take another flight, allowing more fuel to be carried. But I, a man on a mission, get on. The plane, its tanks full, finally takes off into very turbulent headwinds like a flying stick of dynamite. Sleep is out of the question, of course. At takeoff I'm quaking in my steerage-class seat.

Hours and hours later I'm still awake when we cross the international date line and 4:00 A.M. Saturday becomes 3:00 A.M. Sunday in the cold black air above the Pacific. (Another weekend shot to hell.) There's no use gauging time by sunsets and sunrises anymore—much less setting my watch—so I begin marking time by the length of the hair on my unshaven face. I've got a fine, grungy thirty-hour growth and red, sleepless eyes and economy-class clothing when I finally stumble before the immigration officer at the Sydney airport. The plane was in the air thirteen hours and forty-eight minutes.

I'm way down in Australia, but I still have a long way to go.

There's another layover in Sydney, then the interminable final five-hour flight to Perth on the west coast. More airplane food. More airplane air. More airplane babies crying. More worthless airplane Twinkie pillows.

I'm a danger to myself and others when I finally arrive in Perth. Somehow I hail a taxi and drop myself onto a hotel bed. I sleep for almost twenty-four hours straight.

I arise midmorning the next day to a sparkling, sun-blasted, youthful Australian city of skyscrapers where every tenth car has a surfboard strapped on top. I'm here! As advertised, it's summertime and everything's backward. People drive on the wrong side of the road and the steering wheel is on the right. I rent a car and I feel like I'm driving in a mirror. When I signal to turn, I switch on my windshield wipers instead. Every time.

I head south toward tiny Augusta, Australia, the town nearest Cumberland Rock. It's just north of Cape Leeuwin, on the southwestern tip of the continent, 187 miles from Perth. Along the way I stop to watch fairy penguins wobble under the Indian Ocean sun, and I visit a vineyard just north of Augusta. Banish all thought of barren Australian desert here. The soil is rich, giving rise to vineyards and surrounding forests of giant, exotic eucalyptus trees.

I pull into Augusta, population eight hundred, in late afternoon and head straight for a gravel road my maps say will take me up to an ocean overlook. I want to see Cumberland Rock. I'm dying to see Cumberland Rock. In my mind it's become famous, like the Roman Colosseum or the Eiffel Tower, after so many weeks of thinking about it and looking at it on maps. When I do see the rock, two miles out in a haze of afternoon light off a coast as beautiful as anything in Northern California, I'm simultaneously thrilled and horrified. At last, the farthest place in the world from Washington, D.C.! But there, too, is the crashing white foam of waves smashing the crag's steep edges on all sides, over and over again, water spewing everywhere.

There's no way I'll get up there. No way in the world. I'm sure of it.

Crestfallen, I drive back into Augusta. The town is composed basically of a bank, a grocery store, four churches, two restaurants, a few hotels, a liquor store, two gas stations, and a fishmonger. If you blink, you miss it—and I blink. Before turning around, though, I see a wooden sign shaped like a penguin that says Last Eating House Before the Antarctic. It points left.

I dutifully flip on my windshield wipers and proceed to a cafe and bait shop owned by forty-five-year-old Wendy Ferris. I order fish and chips and tell Wendy why I've come. Her suddenly saucer eyes tell me I'm a madman to have traveled so far for such a frivolous reason. But soon she catches the odd contagion of my quest, telling me that Andrew at the hardware store dives for lobsters near Cumberland Rock and might be able to take me there.

Wendy says she had no idea Augusta was on the other side of the world from Washington. I ask her what comes to mind when she thinks of the U.S. capital. Her response is similar to that of everyone I ask in this town where the sea keeps things warm year-round and it never, ever snows: "Bloody freezing cold, I should think."

I drive up to Augusta Hardware and Scuba Supplies and catch Andrew Court and his crew just returning from a day of lobster diving. They're around back, washing down equipment, storing wet suits, and drinking Jim Beam and cola from cans. On the ground are two tubs full of monstrous west Australian rock lobsters weighing as much as thirteen pounds each.

"Washington, D.C.?" Andrew bellows when I introduce myself. "Bloody freezing cold there, I should think." He bursts into laughter, then feigns sudden concern. "Are you having trouble walking around down here, mate? You're upside down, you know. Hang on tight!" More laughter. Another draw of bourbon.

Andrew, thirty-two, a former Australian-rules football player, is the rugged, handsome skipper of the *Lady Leeuwin,* a thirty-foot fishing and diving boat. When he's not taking tourists from Perth out whale-watching or fishing for pink snapper, he dives for rock lobster, mostly for his own table.

45

Andrew quickly gives me three reasons why I probably won't get up on Cumberland Rock. One, the wind and waves will prevent an approach. Two, the rock is steep, slippery, and partially covered with barnacles that will slice flesh like razor blades. Three, the colony of eight New Zealand fur seals there might decide not to let anyone on their rock.

"But we can give it a shot, mate," he says. Then he adds: "As far as I know, no human being's ever been up that rock. You'd be the first. Why not? Be here tomorrow at six A.M."

I camp that night outside Augusta in a eucalyptus forest carpeted with strange giant ferns. The horrifying screech of a kookaburra wakes me at two. I step out of my tent to pee and find myself surrounded by more than a dozen large kangaroos munching away per their nocturnal habit. I go to sleep hoping none of them jumps on me.

At six-thirty the next morning, Andrew unmoors the *Lady Leeuwin* at Hamelin Bay, nine miles north of Cumberland Rock. A crew of four lobster divers and I pile in. A historical marker on the shore gets my attention. It details the maze of old shipwrecks strewn along this rocky coast. The wind is stiff, whipping up small whitecaps. It might be this way all day, Andrew tells me, clearly trying to reduce my hopes of making it onto the rock.

This will be a regular workday for the crew, and until they are through I'm just along for the ride. Soon we're out to sea, with Andrew and company scuba diving along reefs and coming up with some of the biggest lobsters I've ever seen. The men use special wire nooses for their quarry and have strapped to their ankles six-inch-long diving knives that make them look like pirates.

I stay on deck, scanning the Indian Ocean horizon for humpback whales migrating south to Antarctica for the summer. At least once per hour a small group of bottlenose dolphins swims past the boat.

The wind, meanwhile, doesn't let up. One experienced diver eventually gets seasick from all the bouncing. I judge it merciful that our view of Cumberland Rock is blocked all morning by a jag of coastline.

Reef after reef, the diving goes on and I get a little bored and impatient. I've traveled for more than three days and twelve thousand miles—halfway around the world—and now a friendly group of lobster pirates with funny nooses is all that stands between me and my final destination. I put on a wet suit for the chilly water and begin snorkeling for lobsters myself—without luck—hoping to speed up the daily catch.

Suddenly, around eleven o'clock, something truly remarkable happens.

The wind disappears almost entirely. Andrew can't believe it. An hour passes. Still no wind. "I don't think it's coming back," he says. The crew starts whooping. The calm sea makes their work easier, more pleasant. "We haven't had a day like this in a month!" Andrew says. Then he turns to me.

"You have *no idea* how lucky you are. *No idea.* You just might make it up onto your rock."

At twelve-thirty, the lobster catch complete, we weigh anchor and head south. My impatience quickly turns to nervousness. Soon the rock is in view in the distance. Drawing closer, it looks like a fractured stone tortoise shell, sad and all alone at sea. Then, suddenly, I realize something's wrong. There's still white water foaming up around the rock's edges. The surrounding reef is causing a swell that generates turbulence even without wind. "It's still a lot better than usual," Andrew assures me.

We're almost there. Five hundred feet away, we drop anchor. Andrew and I and three other divers—including Mailes, Andrew's first mate—jump into the dinghy, which we'll use to make the final approach. All my senses are trained on the rock. Already we can see and hear the seals. Four are sunning themselves on a ledge above the water. Four more are in the water, swimming, heads popping up to inspect us. The rock looks much bigger up close, like a small island.

Four hundred feet. Three hundred feet. Two hundred. Andrew stops the dinghy. He and Mailes are scratching their chins, contemplating an approach strategy. The trick now is to find a place to climb up onto the rock, and neither seaman looks very happy. We circumnavigate it once, then again. The western side, facing the open sea, is thrashed by waves. The eastern side, where the seals are, is problematically steep. Then Andrew points to a small horizontal ledge five feet above the water on the eastern side.

"There," he says. "That's the only place. Watch the swell."

Every few minutes a big slow wave rolls in and rises up to the ledge's level. "I'll gun the dinghy up the next swell," Andrew says, "then you jump off the bow and onto the ledge."

I thought he was joking until first mate Mailes says, "Look, I'll go first." Mailes crouches on the bow while Andrew waits for the next swell. Then Andrew guns the outboard and we're riding up a slope of water. At the exact right moment, the only moment possible, Mailes jumps with extreme caution, legs spread, knees bent, his whole body hunkered forward. Then he lands. He doesn't fall. The sea doesn't wash him away. He grabs onto the rock and yells back to the dinghy, which is now sliding away: "It's no problem. It's not so slippery. Just be careful of the barnacles. They'll cut you to ribbons. Watch your timing. Don't fall."

Everyone in the dinghy turns to me. I've come all this distance—and now the last thirty feet of the journey look like the longest leg by far. But I can't stop now. I swallow my worries. I climb onto the hull and Andrew waits for the next swell. Then he revs the motor and I have a moment of extreme fright.

But then I jump—and I'm on the rock. It's over. I'm standing up, feeling a thick layer of barnacles under my wet-suit boots. I scramble up the rock to get away from the swell. The seals, twenty feet away, wrinkle their noses then slither into the water. I look down at the dinghy. Andrew and company are cheering and clapping their hands. My adrenaline subsides enough for me to savor, at last, my arrival.

I turn toward the open sea and I feel, quite intensely, the geography of my situation. All of Australia is behind me. The vast Indian Ocean is before me. I'm as far from Washington, D.C., as I can possibly be on solid land. Beneath my feet, below the crust, the mantle, the earth's core, more mantle, more crust, are my home, my wife, my child. Both the North Pole and the South Pole are closer to Washington than this rock is. Tierra del Fuego and Upper Siberia are closer than this rock. The only way to be farther from Washington and have solid ground under your feet is to be on the moon.

I explore the rock, walking toward its western tip. At the center, I find a hidden miniature canyon with a pool of calm seawater at the bottom. It's full of reef crabs and abalone. I enter the canyon and am surrounded completely by stone walls, with only the blue sky above me, the sound of the outer surf gone. I scramble out and then up to the highest point of the rock, on the westernmost tip, facing the ocean. There I place a memento of my visit: a three-inch-wide marble carving of the U.S. Capitol purchased at Washington's Union Station, on the other side of the world, just before my trip.

I stay only about thirty minutes, leaving the same way I came, jumping off the rock and onto the wave-riding dinghy. But before I go I just stand there on the highest point of the rock and relish my moment. It's not Everest, but it's something. All the local fishermen say no human being's ever been on this rock, meaning no human being's ever been so far from D.C. I like Washington, but for a moment, with a faint breeze in my face and the sound of seals behind me, I feel like I never want to leave this place. I've traveled to the end of the Earth, and the feeling is of another world entirely. Better than any fantasy I've had.

For the moment, I'm really here: far, far from home.

5
Tramping Across Sicily

In short order, we've cleaned the abandoned Sicilian farmhouse enough to unfurl our sleeping bags. We place the bags atop a thick mattress of grass and wild flowers picked from right outside the farmhouse door. The windows and door of this one-room peasant's dwelling have long since fallen from their hinges, allowing the light of a burned-red sunset to fill the room. The light pours in from across a landscape of soft rolling hills studded with olive groves and endless vineyards and fields of spring hay.

We dust off a wooden table and bench not used in at least thirty years, then munch on Sicilian almonds and dried apricots. We build a roaring fire in the farmhouse hearth fueled by the grapevine prunings of dusty farmers who, with their gray caps and short tobacco pipes, have all gone home for the day. In the fire's lingering glow, we lay on our sleeping bags and stare up through the missing farmhouse roof at a billion stars blinking on in the night sky. Neither Jim, my companion, nor I can recall a cozier, more beautiful "hotel" in all our travels.

We fall asleep on this hilltop in the middle of the countryside to the lonely whistle of an ancient wind, one that brought the galleys of old mariners—Phoenicians, Greeks, Carthaginians, Romans, Arabs, Normans—to this same Italian island of wild beauty and rustic traditions, a land much closer to Tunis, Tunisia, than to Rome.

But Jim and I are not sailors. We are roaming the countryside on foot—*a piedi*—our goal being to walk sixty miles in one week across the western end of Sicily, from the lemon groves and roaming cattle of the Tyrrhenian Sea coast on the north down to the 2,500-year-old Greek ruins of Selinunte on the Mediterranean Sea to the south. In all of Italy, Sicily is the poorest, most agricultural, most tradition-bound region. What better way, then, to encounter the rural landscape and the colorful peasant farmers, fishermen, and wooden boat builders than, for a while, to become one of them, to tramp like a peasant across the island with all your travel possessions piled high atop your back, leaving you slightly stooped as you walk but with plenty of time to brake and take in the vistas and characters that float into view?

We've come to western Sicily because it's the least developed side of the island . . . and the most African, where people eat couscous and fences are virtually nonexistent; where Arabic-speaking shepherds guide bell-wearing flocks to fields of wild garlic and past freshly tilled rows of yellow-hued cauliflower.

This is not a trip of conventional rewards or comforts. We pass through areas so sparsely populated that, for the locals, just seeing *people* is a rarity, never mind tourists. During one stretch, for two days, we live on handouts of food and local wine, sleeping in beautiful empty farmhouses, there being no villages to go to, no pensiones to stay in, no meals to buy. It is, for us, la dolce vita in the truest sense. We never go hungry and the rural beauty infuses each step with a deep sense of well-being. Almond trees bloom with fragrant, creamy flowers all around us. The early spring sun never stops shining. Scarved women tend hillside vineyards below cottony clouds drifting lazily, like us, in the direction of Africa.

For six days we travel this way, following dirt lanes and paved roads and footpaths south. We wander through hay fields and across vineyards, choosing our way sometimes by complete whim.

I've been to Europe before, including Italy several times, but never like this, never on foot, never here.

We walk, for six days, through a painting.

"You won't be needing a ride back?" asks the taxi driver in Italian, wrinkling his nose with curiosity at our overloaded backpacks.

"No," I say for the third time. "We're on foot from here."

The driver has brought us an hour west of Palermo to San Vito lo Capo, a lovely beach town of barely three thousand off-season inhabitants on the Tyrrhenian Sea coast. The mountains here are straight out of a postcard from Rio de Janeiro: towering stone uplifts that plunge with improbable steepness and beauty right into the sapphire Tyrrhenian Sea.

"*Va bene,*" says the driver finally, gesturing in good Italian fashion to the mountains and sea. "Have a good journey."

We stash our packs in an old hotel with a painted donkey cart in the hallway. The architecture here recalls Sicily's Arab past: blocky stucco buildings with flat roofs and arched doorways of tufa limestone. Dwarf palms and eucalyptus trees adorn hidden piazzas, and the only thing missing is the muezzin's wailing call to prayer.

That night, our first dinner in Sicily is interrupted by lots of shouting from a card game in the back room of an old bar. Men in sweater vests and crisply ironed shirts are playing *scopa,* a local game whose first rule, according to the official rule book, is "always try to see your opponent's cards." So all the artful chaos and charm of Sicilian culture fills our ears as we finish our sidewalk meal of prosciutto sandwiches and Peroni beer, comforted by the soft background crash of ocean surf just a block away.

The next morning, hoisting backpacks whose bungee cords hold both sleeping bags and fresh loaves of sesame bread, we follow the narrow streets out of town, heading south. In minutes we're in the countryside, passing small farmhouses with terra cotta roofs and prickly pear hedges, lemon groves and wandering roosters. In meadows along the two-lane road, delicate stalks of wild fennel grow interspersed with starbursts of yellow flowers the Sicilians call *caladuci*. Jim, a photographer by trade, slips into a dream state full of clicking and focusing and happy sighs.

Two miles out of town, with the Tyrrhenian Sea now panoramically displayed below us, we hear the melodic tones of an enormous, elaborate wind chime. The sound grows stronger and more lovely with each step, its source a mystery to us until finally the scene unfolds: Three dozen shaggy sheep are grazing placidly on a hillside pasture, small bells attached to their collars, their shepherd apparently fast asleep nearby under the warm spring sun. The wonderful chiming fills our ears, saturates the hillside, serenades the sea, and I realize that even on bicycles we might have been going too fast to catch this scene. Some pleasures—and there will be many on this trip—come only to travelers who choose to move no faster than the sheep they encounter.

We break for lunch in the shade of an almond grove, eating cheese and bread and olives cured in garlic, plus lemons picked from trees along the way. After lunch, we strike off on a secondary dirt road and soon meet seventy-five-year-old Francesco San Clemente. He's high atop a homemade ladder in the upper branches of an olive tree. He's holding a bow saw attached to a rope.

"What are you doing?" I ask him in Italian, giving him time to recover from the shock of seeing two Americans wander right up to his tree from out of nowhere.

"I'm making the olive trees wake up," he says proudly, looking down at us in his drab farm clothes, stubble beard, and weathered, bandaged hands. "The trees have been sleeping all winter and if I prune the branches just right, they will wake up and produce very well."

Francesco's been a farmer all his life, he says. "But there's no money in farming," he adds. "I make enough to survive, that's all." Yet on an island where unemployment is 20 percent, where jobs are so scarce that it's against the law to have two, he's not complaining. "When I die, I can be proud. I worked everyday," he says.

This peasant farmer has only one question for us: "Why are you walking?"

"So we can meet the people like you," I say, "who make the olive trees wake up from their long sleep."

We walk twelve miles that first day, down the San Vito Cape, across several lovely valleys, around Mount Cofano. It's late afternoon when we stop for a restorative beer in the small village of Purgatory, where none of the locals knows how the town got its name.

Another hour takes us to the hilltop village of Custonaci and a white-washed hotel separated from the town by a meadow and winding cow path. The view of the now distant Tyrrhenian Sea is lovely from our balcony window past dark-green pine groves and dwarf palms. But this is the only hotel—and restaurant—for a twenty-five-mile stretch of coast, so our expectations are not especially high as we order the *Pasto Completo* that night from Andrea Oado, the proprietor and cook.

Anyone who's eaten very well in continental Italy—as I have—will be skeptical of the guidebook claims that the food is even better, much better, in Sicily. Andrea's gloomy dining area seems a particularly unlikely spot for genius. Only two other parties drift in the whole night. But when Andrea and his daughters Angela and Catarina bring out the white wine and the first of seven courses, our doubts begin to fade.

The antipasto alone makes the table groan: pickled eggplant, cubes of salted tuna, sardines, fresh tomato slices, eggplant stewed with raisins, almonds, and pine nuts. Then comes a plate of delicately, perfectly fried mozzarella cheese. Then spaghetti with a ragu sauce so good (just a hint of anchovies) that by itself it would have made the meal a knockout. Then a large country omelet made with early potatoes, garlic, and onions. Then a pitcher of red wine and the main course of Italian sausage and veal cutlets served with cold celery greens splashed with oil and vinegar. Then huge, whole oranges so fresh the leafy stems are still attached. Then espresso and canoli with smokey-tasting shells.

I can count on one hand the meals I've had this good in my life . . . and I have no fingers at all for the price: $18 per person for everything.

Buonissimo, Signor Oado. *Stupendo,* Catarina. *Mille grazie,* Angela!

Our goal the next day is the city Trapani, thirteen miles away along a winding road that takes us back to the Tyrrhenian Sea coast. We're entering serious wine country now, with vineyards that stretch as far as the eye can see, studded with millions and millions of support posts strung with miles of thin wire. The vineyard posts create that artful visual contrast, so pleasing in the early-morning sun, of row after row of perfectly straight lines spreading over ridge after ridge of unruly, rollicking, curvaceous hills.

Farmers everywhere are tying the gnarled grape stalks to the support wires for the upcoming season. We meet Gaspere Tedesco, a farmer in his seventies who seems suspiciously drunk. Tucked under the belt of his dirty trousers are hundreds of precut elastic strips for tying vines. Gaspere sways slightly as he admits that all that tying is tedious work. But he likes the peacefulness of the vineyard, he says.

"Is the wine from this vineyard very good?" I ask him.

"Of course," he says.

"Do you ever drink some of it while you work?"

"Of course," he says, and totters back to work.

By lunch we're back on the coast, breathing salt air and watching fishermen wade into the water with rakes to hunt sea urchins. Farther out, men wearing wool turtlenecks and shark-tooth necklaces set nets from wooden rowboats. The boat oars are beautiful things, lovingly painted sky blue. They glisten, wet, under the Sicilian sun.

Just outside Trepan, deeply tired, we throw off our packs along a sandy beach and take a breather next to Signor Marino Giuseppe, an itinerant roadside Madonna salesman. Marino's rusting truck, rear doors thrown wide open, is full of cheap, three-foot-tall plaster statues of the Madonna, ten bucks each. He also has statues of Padre Pio, various angels, and Botticelli's Venus.

"Most people, they buy the Madonna," Marino says, "but infertile women, they come to me and buy the Venus and put it in their house and in six months they are pregnant. Guaranteed."

We hitchhike the last mile into Trapani, a city of seventy thousand people right on the sea with an old quarter as beautiful as anything in Naples or Rome. We pass cobblestone piazzas and narrow side streets hung with laundry before reaching an ancient hotel built by the Spanish three hundred years ago. The place needs paint and the stairwell handrails come loose at the touch. But the sign out front insistently proclaims *Albergo Moderno*, Modern Hotel.

After two days in the countryside, Trapani seems like a huge metropolis to us. We marvel at the wealthy Sicilians dressed stylishly in black clothes from head to toe, browsing store windows full of chinaware and fine men's hats. We dash into bars for quick espressos standing up and eat couscous with stuffed squid and spaghetti drenched in cuttlefish ink at a restaurant by the sea.

We rest our backs and legs the next day, casually exploring Trapani's streets. We visit the old fish market under a pavilion of medieval architecture along a harbor that's been a magnet to foreign invaders for centuries. The market itself recalls every chaotic, bustling Arab suq from Tangier to Amman. Octopuses squirm inside wooden crates. Fishmongers in knit caps proclaim the freshness of their eels (three varieties), shrimp (four varieties), clams, mussels, oysters, sea urchins, and fish I've never seen before: green, red, spiny, armored.

The banter between sellers and regulars is practiced and humorous.

"Your fish aren't fresh today," says one customer.

"Not fresh?" says the monger.

"No."

"Well . . . your wife has horns!"

"Your fish have horns!"

It's March eighth, Ash Wednesday, and in this consummately Catholic region we feel duty bound to attend evening mass. Trapani's San Lorenzo cathedral is characteristically massive and ornate and, when we arrive, full of Sicilian faithful who are fasting that day. Amid fourteen interior pillars that rise up toward medieval sculptures of cherubs and paintings of Christ's crucifixion, the priest invites everyone to form a line to receive ashes. Unlike America, where you get an ashen smudge on your forehead, the robed, tall-hatted priest here simply dumps a thimbleful right on your head.

As I approach the priest, I see those before me, already seated: women with ashes in their hair, bald men with small piles on their pates, nuns with ashy habit tops. I bow for my sprinkling and take my seat.

A Sicilian carpenter later tells me: "It's to remember we came from ashes and to ashes we will go. So don't worry so much. Enjoy your life."

We leave the coast early the next morning, striking out on foot across western Sicily's panoramic inland countryside. We point ourselves toward the southeast and the Mediterranean Sea, a three-day walk away. Naively, we are supplied with only a couple of sandwiches and a few Power Bars, unaware that the world before us is so rural and isolated that for two days there will be no opportunities to buy food of any kind and even drinking water will be hard to find.

All we know that first morning is that it's a pluperfect spring day and we're hopelessly lost within an hour of our hike. Our map is wrong, the roads all screwy, so we follow a dirt lane that seems to go in the right direction until we bump into a young Tunisian shepherd and his hundred head of sheep. The concept of fences hasn't taken hold in most of Sicily, meaning shepherds are still very much necessary. Many Sicilian land owners bring in Tunisians by ferry from 120 miles away to work for as little as $10 a day. But this particular shepherd can't help us. He can't read maps, he says. Doesn't understand them.

We're still lost.

We press on, walking deeper into a landscape that gets more beautiful with each mile. Vineyards spread to the summits of low hills on either side of the road. Scattered pastures and olive groves and fields of mature cabbage add their own decorative patches to the quiltlike softness of the land.

In the air hangs the faint smell of wild garlic and freshly plowed earth. The richness serves to remind that the very name Sicily meant fertile land to the ancients.

Later we stop a farmer with sunburned cheeks and a wool cap sitting atop a tractor, and I'm amazed: He can't read the map either, just doesn't understand that the triangular island before him is *his* Sicily. Farther down the road, another farmer not only can't read the map, he can't speak Italian. He speaks only Sicilian, the island's fading dialect. We're really entering the sticks now.

Finally, we reach a paved road that conforms to our map in a valley where workers are busily harvesting bunches of cauliflower. Jim and I take a respite and watch as men with sharp knives and striped shirts stack the bunches along the road for pickup. I'd read that Sicily is a land of enduring superstitions, where, for example, the number 17 is considered very unlucky and high-rises in Palermo have no seventeenth floor. But it's still a surprise to hear one of the field hands count the cauliflower bunches: ". . . fourteen, fifteen, sixteen, sixteen plus one, eighteen . . ."

We push on, intrigued by the sudden plethora of small, abandoned farmhouses all around, some centuries old. The houses are made of stone with terra-cotta shingle roofs, shaded by a wild olive tree or two. Each looks like a still-life painting of old, romantic Italian life. But they are empty, these buildings, most without doors and windows, the old feudal system of small plots tended by landless peasants having collapsed in the last century. We later pass a castle with towers and battlements, completely abandoned, unmarked, and gathering moss.

Under today's modern system, farmers with trucks and tractors tend huge tracts of land and live in widely spaced towns too far away for us to reach easily on foot. So when sunset comes, we pick a particularly lovely old farmhouse on a particularly lovely hill and move in. After sweeping, salvaging a table, making a mattress of grass, and gathering firewood, we explore a nearby barn full of hitching posts and troughs for horses, an empty wine cask, and pieces of a rusty plow. We imagine the workworn parents who once lived here, their children in threadbare clothes, their grandchildren perhaps Brooklyn bakers or Philadelphia lawyers now, having joined the million Sicilian poor who've emigrated to America in the last 120 years.

Tucked inside this ancestral home, surrounded by hovering memories, we build a fire in the long-unused hearth as the last of the evening sun deserts rose-hued vineyards all around us. Jim and I eat a simple dinner befitting of peasants and drift off.

The next morning we have a problem: We're in the middle of nowhere and we're completely out of food and almost out of water. A two-hour hike south puts us five miles closer to our ultimate goal of the Mediterranean Sea but no closer to food or drink. Then, right on time, a large winery appears before us. It's a farmers' cooperative belonging to local producers. Inside a modern of-fice, Giuseppe, the chain-smoking manager, disappoints me: "We have no drinking water," he says. "It's all gone. But we *do* have lots of wine. You may have noticed. Want some?"

"Sure." I shrug, unsure but thirsty.

He takes my plastic liter bottle and leads me to a two-story-tall steel vat so large it holds 25,000 liters and has a spiral staircase around it. At the bot-tom is a tiny spigot, and in an act ludicrously out of scale, he fills my bottle free of charge. He then gives me all the food on the premises: a half-dozen sweet oranges.

After a shady brunch of wine and oranges, Jim and I eventually find a roadside spring for water where another kind man gives us more fruit.

Civilization in the form of the large village of Castelvetrano is only a few miles away, but we're tired and half-buzzed from the wine and half-lost. Our map remains stubbornly useless in the countryside, so we abandon the road and take off across vineyards and through pastures and around a lake until we meet a Tunisian shepherd who happily drives us the last few miles into town in an old Fiat whose interior, like the man, smells of sheep.

Suddenly in downtown Castelvetrano, Jim and I stand in a piazza before a shiny shop window and take in our reflections: We're dirty and unshaven, our baseball caps stained with salt, our bodies a bit lean from modest eating and wilted from carrying heavy packs for almost a week. We've become, in appearance at least, *terroni,* "people of the earth," that term northern Italians regularly apply—with a sniff—to rural Sicilians.

But we're not finished. Astonishingly, in this town of thirty thousand people, there are no hotels. Not one. After coffee and sandwiches, Jim decides to take a bus the last nine miles to the Mediterranean Sea town of Selinunte and a guaranteed pensione.

But I'm committed to seeing this thing through. With the sun setting fast, I hike out of Castelvetrano and soon have my pick of abandoned farmhouses amid subtle hills blanketed in olive groves. I settle on a lovely little place, build a fire, find some hay for a mattress, and plunge into a deep sleep.

I'm up at first light, covering the last six miles in a damp shroud of fog and low clouds. The countryside grows flatter, the landscape given to blooming almond groves whose billion little petals bear beads of delicate water in the misty haze. The road is empty and the walk is lonely.

By eight o'clock I can see the gray Mediterranean Sea at last, stretching toward the southern horizon. In the foreground, in fantastic silhouette against the water, lay the Greek ruins of Selinunte, getting closer. I see the enormous temple to Hera, its thirty-eight fluted columns arranged in a perfect rectangle, a postcard pose of Parthenonesque beauty by the sea.

I climb a stone wall and amble over to the temple, ascending its steps. Between two towering pillars I throw off my backpack and have a seat, facing the sea. The gates to these ruins don't officially open for another hour. I'm here illicitly, all alone.

Later I'll walk down to the tiny village of Selinunte and dip my toe in the Mediterranean Sea on a beach where fishermen gather to auction their morning catch. But for now I just linger on the temple steps, my long journey almost complete. I measure one of the pillars: Its circumference requires four spans of my arms. Hannibal the Carthaginian destroyed this Greek settlement in 409 B.C., savagely looting and pillaging. He traveled only a few more miles to get here than I did, I suddenly realize. But at least he had a boat.

I stare out into the gray sea as the sun begins to break through the clouds. For a moment, it seems I can almost see Africa.

Almost.

11
Outdoors in America

6

A Wilderness Island in Angry Lake Superior

Captain Mark Nyman spins the boat wheel furiously, guiding his ferry up and over another four-foot swell. It's 9:30 A.M. and the weather report crackles over the wheelhouse radio. A small craft advisory is still in effect for western Lake Superior, with more high winds and high waves expected. But now there's a second advisory for *water spouts*—tornadoes of spinning water that can instantly turn boats into wreckage.

Standing in the wheelhouse, I suddenly see the world as a grainy black-and-white film: all dark skies and whitecapped water, everything bouncing in and out of focus. Captain Nyman scans the horizon for water spouts, then spins the wheel wildly through another swell. Then he notices my greenish pallor. "Did I tell you?" he says. "This is a B.Y.O.B. wheelhouse. Bring your own bucket."

But surely weak knees and an uneasy stomach are to be expected—indeed, are part of the point—when you travel to one of the wildest places in America. Up ahead, fifteen miles away, battered by waves and surrounded by old shipwrecks, is the most remote and least-visited national park in the lower forty-eight states: Isle Royale. In every way, this island is a place of extremes. Forty-five miles long and barely eight miles wide, Isle Royale National Park sits off the extreme northeastern tip of Minnesota in a lake so huge, it alone contains 10 percent of the world's freshwater supply. It's a rambling, rugged patch of north woods wilderness, full of moose and timber wolves, that gets fewer visitors each year—around twenty thousand—than Yellowstone gets in a single *day* during peak season. (The only parks that get fewer visitors are a couple of vast tracts in remote Alaska.) Isle Royale is the only national park without a single public road, and the only one that closes for the winter, shutting down from November to mid-April because boats can't get into its frozen harbors. It's so far north that visitors can watch the flicker of northern lights, and ice clings to the island's northern shore till the Fourth of July.

And, right now, it's getting closer. Spared the menacing water spouts, the ferry rolls and rocks past a final submerged shipwreck and into the shelter of Washington Harbor on the island's western tip. The wind dies down, and the sky, as if on cue, clears enough to scatter sunlight on the brilliant, unbroken forest. It's the first day of October and autumn is in full climax. Mountain ridges carved during the last ice age erupt with red sugar maples and yellow-leafed birch that give the illusion of liquid, tumbling and surging down valleys and over ledges to the craggy shores of Superior. Amid those trees are 1,500-pound bull moose and roving packs of eastern timber wolves—and an isolation so complete that half of the island's seventy-two inland lakes haven't been named. Types of fish and squirrel, cut off from the mainland, are evolving into completely new species.

October brings the fewest visitors to this least-visited park—112 in 1996. The twice-weekly ferry from Grand Portage, Minnesota, is only half-full today with twenty-two hard-core backpackers. The two ferries from Michigan's upper peninsula have already shut down for the season, as has the island's sole seaplane service. And the skeleton park crew is rushing to close shop ahead of the big snows.

Yet everyone who knows Isle Royale agrees that early October—when the colors are peaking and Indian summers are not unknown and the blackflies have stopped biting and the moose are in rut (and thus more visible)—is the very best time to come. And so here I am, backpack in tow, seeking an experience extreme only in its simplicity: I want to be utterly alone in a wild landscape. I want to encounter untrammeled nature in an unmediated way; to behold an environment as different as possible from my urban world where my toddler's first—and most-repeated—sound is that of a siren. The idea's not original, but going solo in a place this remote is, for me, a first.

To seal the deal, I've gone one step further. In this scarcely known wilderness during maximum low season, I've staked out the island's most remote region, its southwest corner. I'll hike thirty miles in four days without seeing another human being. Through sunny afternoons and freezing nights I'll manage on my own while wolves leave tracks around my campsites and maple leaves flutter to the ground to the laughter of migrating loons breaking camp for points south.

I bed down my first night in a spruce and fir forest, not far from my ferry drop on the island's western end. After sunset, I hear the bellowing snorts and grunts of several moose in rut. The weird noise echoes through the woods around me. I can't see the animals, but I hear sticks snapping under their mighty hooves and against their mighty antler racks. I pray the moose don't stumble too close to my tent.

Henry David Thoreau had a specific definition of "wild" in mind when he penned his line, "In wildness is the preservation of the world." In one of his journals Thoreau writes, "Wild—past particle of *to will*, self-willed." The world, Thoreau seems to say, is only in harmony when animals, plants, landscape, *and* man are self-willed and self-determinate together, wild and free at the same spot.

These thoughts are on my mind as one-ton mammals, drunk with desire, wander about my defenseless, prostrate frame. I've left city concrete and smothering social conventions to be around animals and elements that are self-willed, and where I might even be at their mercy. From the pitched boat ride forward, this is a trip about exchanging control for something else.

It's not a romantic proposition, nor do I expect romance. Already I'm cold, my breath billowing through twenty-nine-degree night air, and the moose won't stop snorting long enough to let me sleep. It goes on and on, the racket, and by midnight I yearn for a switch to throw or a noise cop to call. My desire to manipulate dies hard in this remote wilderness until suddenly I laugh at the very idea: remote control.

I wake the next morning to a dream state born of sleep deprivation and the dawn of a pluperfect autumn day. There's not a cloud in the cobalt sky and by ten o'clock I'm in shirtsleeves atop a ridge, sitting on my pack, looking over a third of Isle Royale awash in blinding sunlight with the deep blue of Lake Superior spreading to the horizon. There are 165 miles of trails on this island, enough for all my fellow ferry passengers to go their separate ways, leaving virtually all of what's before me—a succession of red-and-gold valleys, watery cedar swamps, rocky shorelines—utterly empty of Gore-Tex-clad creatures. I set off again, my boots crunching fallen aspen leaves, and the scale of my presence suddenly thrills me.

I hike till noon, stopping for lunch atop a beaver-felled tree in a cedar swamp. Perhaps nothing marks wilderness more than its stillness, its silence—and the quietude of this swamp borders on startling. A soft breeze blows through the trees and I can literally hear the hushed landing of falling pine needles.

As in most journeys into natural settings, everything and nothing happens at the same time. A red fox crosses my path, a cool sweat gathers between my shoulder blades, a bald eagle circles, I run my hand over a swatch of grandfather's beard lichen on a rock. Signs of wolves and moose are everywhere. I see prints. I see scat. But I don't see the animals. They are choosing not to reveal themselves, asserting their will, being wild—but I know they're there.

A Wilderness Island in Angry Lake Superior

After nine miles I reach Lake Feldtmann, a four-hundred-acre body of blue forged by long-ago glaciers and enclosed by violently beautiful autumn foliage. I gawk at the lake's glassy surface and shoreside beds of delicate pencil reeds. I make camp near the south shore, then assemble my fishing rod, hoping to test my skills against the three-foot northern pikes said to lurk here.

But the lake is shallow, and to get at the fish I have to wade in barefoot and—with no people around—minus pants. At about sixty degrees, the water is actually much warmer than the air around me, which has turned suddenly colder with a burst of clouds and wind from the northwest. Comfortably warm from my naked waist down, I'm bundled up above—fleece shirt, sweater, jacket, cap—and I cast awkwardly in wool gloves. The same wind making my teeth chatter has turned the lake to whitecaps, and the fish aren't even thinking about biting. Swamps and underbrush, meanwhile, keep me from the few lake coves sheltered from the wind, and I grow frustrated. I can't win. The lake has willed itself unfishable. It's still this way the next morning when it's time to move on, though I try once more in my absurd Arctic-Bahamas fashion statement.

Two miles down the trail, the wind finally breaks and the sky clears and I'm on a nearby ridge looking down on Lake Feldtmann: a calm, blue, distant pearl begging for an angler's hook. But the day's much too beautiful for regrets, and I rest in a small meadow of blooming white asters, feeling warm and content, admiring the old Objibway Indian name for this island: Minong, a good place to be.

Skirting ridgetops, I hike much of the morning below a bizarre, fifteen-foot-tall, topographically correct stone ledge that is in fact an old shoreline of Lake Superior. Before the retreat of the last glaciers, everything below this line was underwater and the island itself was a fraction of its current size. I have lunch on this old shoreline—now a forested spot way up in the sky—while sitting on a crude stone beach chair pounded into shape by waves ten thousand years ago.

It's now been two days since I've seen another human being in this half-million-acre park, and as I down a handful of trail gorp with absolutely no one to talk to, I already have the answer to what everyone back home will immediately ask me: Weren't you lonely? No. In fact, not only was I not lonely, I never even felt alone. The United Nations declared Isle Royale an International Biosphere Reserve in 1981 owing to its two hundred species of wildflowers (including thirty-two species of orchids), 238 recorded species of birds (including the American black duck and red-breasted merganser), several dozen species of trees, four dozen species of butterflies, and much, much more. With so many riches, the distraction of a second human presence would have meant less time to enjoy it all.

Besides, by the second day I realize I'm having rich conversations with my surroundings—wordless, cyclical exchanges that go something like this: observe, think, touch, smell, listen, observe, think, touch, smell . . .

I reach Siskiwit Bay on the island's south side in late afternoon, bone weary after what's now twenty miles in two days with my thirty-five-pound pack. I crumple to the ground before a bay drenched in golden October light with spruce boughs casting long shadows over calm water drifting in from Superior. Before me, a couple of adult loons, already in grayish winter plumage, make their famously awkward aquatic takeoff, walking then running atop the water until finally getting airborne and pointing themselves south, their long migration begun. If the last of these birds don't leave the island soon, they'll be stranded by winter ice, unable to get a running start across open water.

Unlike Lake Feldtmann, where some stretches of the shore looked as if packs of big German shepherds had been running about, I see no wolf tracks along the curving shore of Siskiwit Bay. One of my goals had been to see a wolf or moose in the wild. As for the latter, I've heard them snorting everywhere, seen the aspen trees they denude for food, seen their scattered bones left by attacking wolves, and even seen a moose love site—a confusion of hoofprints on the trail (one set bigger, one smaller) bunched in a wild circle, with some dug in deeply, presumably for extra traction. I've even *smelled* a couple of musty old moose. But no visual contact. Instead of being disappointed by this fact, I'm increasingly thrilled. The moose and wolves seem more wild to me with each passing day, skulking in the shadows of the forest just beyond my detection. Self-willed, free, untamed—they are utterly unconcerned with my petty voyeur's agenda.

Today, even before sunset, I can feel it's going to be a cold night. My ungloved hands are freezing as I set up my tent. I crawl into my sleeping bag wearing my wool hat, gloves, and heavy coat—and I mentally visualize all those blue "blasts" of Arctic air on TV weather maps that pass through customs not far from Isle Royale.

The next day, the bay is an angry howl of waves and ear-blasting wind coming straight off Lake Superior. I boil the last of my water for coffee. The only source of water now is the bay itself. Not wanting to get soaked, I look at a map, locating Caribou Creek a mile away where it enters the bay along the hiking trail. But for all of that mile-long stretch the trail is the bay shore, and I'm completely exposed to the wind and the den of crashing waves. I feel bullied by a landscape gone slightly mad. When I finally reach Caribou Creek, I cringe: It has willed itself dry except for a few rancid puddles. From here the trail veers toward dry ridges. I need water now.

I look back at the bay. If I roll up my pants above the knees and wade out just a short distance beyond the backwash, I should be all right. But of course it's only seconds before I'm ambushed by a big wave and soaked to my waist. Blue as an icicle, I race back to my pack and hurriedly strip off my pants—at which point a gust of wind blows stinging sand all over my wet legs and sends my baseball cap tumbling down the shore again. I go racing after the hat in my clinging wet boxers, stepping on sharp sticks in my bare feet. That's when I hear the moose.

I can't see him, but he has to be close for me to hear his grunts above the wind. I'm convinced he's watching me, secretly pleased by the sight of a thirsty, half-naked, freezing human hopping and yelping, teeth chattering, down the shore after a tumbling hat. The moose snorts again, fainter now that I'm moving away, as if to say, "You want wilderness? We got your wilderness."

The planned hike today is blessedly short, offsetting the eternity it takes to get dry, warm, and sufficiently sand-free to walk again. Despite the ordeal I feel strong this morning, the rhythm of my walk more sure after three days on the trail. I'm heading deeper into the island's interior, moving through glorious climax forests of red oaks and red maples. I feel my connection to the island deepen in rough parallel. In a grassy meadow I find fantastically tall dandelion plants and pick their leaves to supplement my dinner. I find wild basil to accent the chili I'll eat tonight.

I camp in a gray birch forest in a saddle between two ridges. This natural shelter allows me to forgo a tent, and dusk finds me out in the open, eating my gathered leaves and chili as stars blink on overhead and the moose begin their nightly ruckus. I climb into my sleeping bag rubbing the lengthening whiskers on my dirty face, and with nothing to shield me I stare at silvery moonlight pouring down everywhere through autumn branches rapidly losing their leaves. For a moment, the almost-full moon, rife with ancient mystery and luminescent power, makes me want to scream and shout and do a pagan dance. But fatigue catches up with me and I drift off to a dark sleep instead. The sound of the distant moose on the prowl no longer bothers me at all.

I've . . . adapted.

On the fourth day I come down from the wilderness. I follow the gradual descent of the Greenstone Ridge, so named for the semiprecious "green star stone" found here. Barely a mile from the ferry dock where my hike began four days before, it finally happens: I see a moose. An enormous bull with a towering rack steps onto the trail two hundred feet ahead of me. He eyes me blankly. He's at least seven feet tall from hoof to antler. I'm thrilled, but a little perplexed when the bull doesn't move. I sit on my pack and we just stare at each other until I hear a loud grunt behind me. Sure enough it's a cow, on the trail and getting closer. "Don't *ever, ever, ever* get between a cow and a bull moose in rut," all the guidebooks say. "The bull might take you for competition and charge like an angry tank."

In no time I'm up a hill and behind a tree, peeking down as the bull and cow hoof it toward each other until their noses touch. After a moment of mutual inspection, they have the decency to drift off into the forest, allowing me to go my way, grinning at how their consummation offers my trip its own.

Back at Washington Harbor, I wait atop the ferry dock made of rocks and cedar logs with a beaver living underneath. When the ferry captain arrives he's eager to depart immediately for the two-and-a-half-hour trip back to Minnesota. A gale is forecast for later that afternoon, with waves an astonishing ten feet. With a handful of other backpackers, I climb aboard, eyeing everyone with something akin to fascination: *people.*

Bouncing across the open water of Lake Superior, with Isle Royale shrinking in the distance like a fragile remembrance, I go below deck to the ship's water closet. Someone's left a mirror inside and I take a peek, quite alarmed by my sun- and wind-burned cheeks, my cracking chapped lips, my Don King hair.

And that smell? Sweat, dirt, smoke, sour clothes, mountain air, a hint of pine. Is that what freedom smells like? Was Thoreau this overpowering?

7
Amazing Grace in the Texas Desert

P eople who spend lots of time on rivers agree, with little dissent, that
these coursing bodies of water have spirits. They are alive. Treat them
well, respect them, and rivers will grant you safe passage over rough
rapids and through narrow canyons. Disrespect them and beware. It is almost
a given, for example, that any canoeist who brags he's never flipped his boat
on a certain cataract will, the very next time, flip his boat on that cataract.

So it's uncertain what terrible thing I—or my guides—did to upset one of
the wildest, most beautiful river canyons you've never heard of: Santa Elena
Canyon deep inside Big Bend National Park along Texas's Rio Grande. Who
knows why that freak event happened when it did, the way it did—an act of
God that almost killed us by means few people will ever believe.

But it happened. And there are several witnesses. And maybe it's not so amazing after all. For if there exists anywhere on Earth a place big enough and wild enough and empty enough to harbor forces completely beyond our comprehension, it is here in the Chihuahuan Desert of western Texas, an expanse of sand, canyons, and mountains the size of Maryland with an unfathomably small human population of thirteen thousand lonely souls. Big Bend National Park forms the beating heart of that boundless desert world with 1,200 square miles of scrub bushes and roadrunners and rattlesnakes hard by the Mexican border along an eponymous southernly dip of the Rio Grande.

Here stand the "Phantom" Mountains, the final wilderness bastion of fight-to-the-end Apache Indians. Their ghosts still roam free amid mountain lions and wild horses and black bears across desert peaks soaring to almost eight thousand feet. On the surrounding desert floor, stretching away infinitely in all directions, weird shadows and blinding sunlight play tricks with your eyes until sunsets of lavender-rose incandescence finally break your heart.

Though endearing to the human imagination, this desert is hostile in every other way, safeguarding its secrets with no fewer than eleven species of stinging scorpions, a plethora of giant tarantulas, a near total lack of water, and a labyrinth of cactuses whose thorns range in name from "horse crippler" to "eagle's claw." No wonder so few people have ever even heard of the desert rat here that never drinks water or the strikingly wind-carved Indian faces on desert buttes or the mysterious clouds of white light appearing late at night, over and over again, on the desert floor, with no explanation whatsoever. (Note: These queer lights outside of Marfa, Texas, have been documented and videotaped to death—unlike every UFO you've ever heard of.)

Yet across this ghostly desert landscape where normal laws simply don't apply, the sanctum sanctorum of oddity is surely that appalling fracture in the earth called Santa Elena Canyon. Below her fifteen-hundred-foot sheer cliff walls the world has no horizon and water flows uphill and river rafts miraculously fit through rock doors narrower than the width of the rafts themselves. The Rio Grande here took a cool one hundred million years to plow through an entire range of mountains called today the Mesa of Eels, and the river twists and bends just like the slithering namesake. Just downstream from this remotest of remote spots, rumors fly among gringos and Mexicans alike of lost conquistador burial caves, where mad-smiling skeletons lay supine in medieval helmets and full breastplates, gripping swords with bleached, dusty knuckles that once killed and conquered.

It is here, in the middle of Santa Elena Canyon, in a sixteen-foot raft named *Sun Dog*, that the strange thing in question happened. A mile into this giant vault of limestone, just above a series of challenging rapids, we heard the gunshots. They exploded only a few feet away, shattering our ears, sending us ducking for cover and scanning the canyon rim for deadly snipers. But it wasn't guns making that deafening noise that soon had us rowing madly, white as apparitions, mumbling prayers that wafted up the canyon walls.

The assault on your senses begins the moment you leave the airport outside Odessa, Texas, and point yourself south toward the Mexican border, four hours away. There's no fast way to get to Big Bend National Park. It's not near anything or on the way to anywhere.

And getting there means following two-lane gun-barrel roads that take you through a wonderful landscape of true-life cliches: tiny Texas ranch towns full of cowboy-hatted men and squeaking windmill wells, where the only traffic signal is a tilting yellow sign downtown saying Loose Cattle. In the distance, you can literally see a hundred miles to buttes and mesas straight out of Roadrunner cartoonland. The roadrunners themselves are everywhere, scampering across the hot asphalt as you pull over to a roadside burrito shack with Mexican horns spilling from your car radio because Spanish-language frequencies are all you can find. The only thing moving between these infrequent towns are dust devils and lost burros and the occasional U.S. Border Patrol vehicle with giant whip antennae and all-terrain tires.

A lonely park ranger collects my fee at Big Bend's northern entrance around three o'clock, and for a long time I see no one else inside. I pull over, walk a quarter mile into the desert, and stop amid scattered creosote bush, prickly pear cactus, towering yucca, and a violently beautiful arroyo carved by years of flash floods. There is no sound except the trill of a desert cicada and an occasional riffle of wind.

Astronauts have used the dry, rocky terrain of Big Bend to simulate moonscapes. But it's a moonscape teeming with life. There on the desert floor I see darting lizards and the pink flash of a western coachwhip snake. Nothing else moves across this ground that can reach summertime temperatures of 150 degrees, but I know that just beyond sight blacktail jackrabbits hide in the shade of cactuses, their megaphone ears serving as complex air conditioners. In burrows below my feet lie kangaroo rats that never drink water, getting their moisture entirely from food, and expelling a bizarre paste that serves as urine.

I return to my car, sidestepping a fist-size tarantula, and immediately become aware that my arms and ankles are burning. Every guidebook to Big Bend is fairly brimming with the same emphatic warning: Bring tweezers! Almost every plant here—bushes, cactuses, trees, flowers—has some sort of thorn or spine. And my short walk into the desert has left my arms and legs peppered with hairlike, skin-piercing needles of unknown origin, all stubbornly resisting removal by hand. And of course I forgot the tweezers.

Only an astounding sunset drive takes my mind off the stinging and itching. I wend my way up into the Chisos Mountains. The name translates from Apache as "phantom" or "ghost," and the shadowy sunset light indeed gives the mountains a haunted feel. In Green Canyon, I stop to watch three black bears, extremely rare here, scramble up a rocky slope. A ranger later tells me he's been in the park an entire year and never seen a bear. I'm here an hour and I see three—a sign, surely, that unusual things are going to happen on this trip.

High in the mountains, at five thousand feet, I find a small Park Service store in a lovely bowllike basin. Here the air is dramatically cooler and the land greener with pinyon pines and scrub oaks. The store carries mostly backcountry essentials—stove fuel, Power Bars, and, against one wall, an entire rack bulging with tweezers. I buy a pair and go to work on my arms and ankles.

78

Amazing Grace in the Texas Desert

At first light the next morning, I make the five-mile hike to the rocky summit of Emory Peak, the highest of these mountains at 7,825 feet. I pass piglike javelinas and Sierra del Carmen deer along the way, but no people. At the summit, all by myself in a flood of sunlight, I look down on a miraculous scene: a continuous sheet of clouds blankets the desert floor all the way to distant mountain ranges on the Mexican side. I've ascended to heaven. To the east, west, and south lies only Mexico, surrounding this tonguelike peninsula of Texas.

After a while, the clouds to the south open, like curtains, and there it is: the eastern entrance to Santa Elena Canyon. Even from seventeen miles away, those quarter-mile-tall walls look freakishly high and forbidding against the rolling desert floor and the rippling current of the Rio Grande. The rest of the canyon is beyond sight, its body swallowed completely by the earth, as elusive as a whispered rumor.

I begin my approach to the canyon by exiting the park to the west and heading south on two-lane Highway 170 toward tiny Lajitas, Texas, on the Rio Grande. I stop along the way at the only restaurant for miles, Papa Rios, where "bano" is scrawled across a wood-plank bathroom door and cowboys with walrus mustaches sit hunched forward, rolling their own cigarettes after huge Mexican meals.

The desert cactuses are throwing long shadows as I pass through an eerie ghost town outside Lajitas, where moldering adobe buildings once supported a community of quicksilver miners. Minutes later, Lajitas itself seems nearly as deserted. With its Old West false-fronted shops along a dusty boardwalk, this town of thirty people caters mostly to tourists. But since few come, the hotel, quilt shop, country store, and other shops are mostly empty. The town's famous for having been robbed by Pancho Villa's men ninety years ago, and a lot of that anarchist frontier spirit endures. The official mayor is Clay Henry III, the beer-drinking goat. It's election time when I arrive, and fliers supporting Clay Henry—as well as his opponent "The Wooden Indian"—are plastered all along the boardwalk in the style of wanted posters.

The next morning, passing the town's requisite Loose Cattle traffic sign, I meet my river guides on the north bank of the Rio Grande. Head guide Jim Haney and first mate Jason Hodgman quickly settle me and four other passengers—married couples from Georgia and Wisconsin—into two sixteen-foot inflatable rafts with gear. We launch into the slow-moving current, leaving behind a group of barefoot migrant workers still asleep on the Mexican bank.

The cloudy Rio Grande is nothing spectacular here, barely three feet deep and maybe one hundred feet wide. It's pleasantly fringed by river cane and brilliantly green salt cedars, beyond which the contrasting brown dryness of the desert resumes, sprinkled with yucca and cactuses. We're soon officially back inside Big Bend park, which spreads to the horizon to our left while all of Mexico lies to our right. The next trace of human civilization will be a rutted dirt road—a two-day float away—where we'll finally take out.

Jim, deeply tanned behind wraparound sunglasses, is a complete river nut, guiding trips in Washington State in the summer and trips here in the autumn and winter. He camps out maybe 250 nights a year, he says, and his hobby is rafting Class 6 rapids, i.e. water so wild no one's successfully run it before. As a result, he's been repeatedly "Maytagged," caught in underwater spin cycles for dangerously long periods before being spit to the surface. All for kicks.

Thankfully, ours will be a decidedly mellow float, with only a few minor rapids inside Santa Elena Canyon. We'll enter the canyon tomorrow after slowly traversing the desert floor today.

By late morning, exactly as planned, we've fallen off the map, floating through trackless desert in the middle of nowhere. The ghostly Chisos Mountains rise to our left while here and there wild horses appear atop nearby mesas, haughty and beautiful, rearing on hind legs.

The view to the south is particularly striking, where the main body of the Chihuahuan Desert extends four hundred harsh and unforgiving miles into northern Mexico. Hard-core Jim, the guy who's not afraid to get Maytagged, says he gets nervous over on that side of the desert during occasional Jeep treks, praying he doesn't break down.

But here on the river, the feeling is one of ease and complete freedom amid wild and sun-blasted beauty. The information packet for this trip warned: "Don't bring money or watches. You won't need either where you're going." My kind of place. Time stops and amenities are blessedly scarce.

Later we see in the distance a chimneylike butte called the Sentinel, where sculpted Indian faces keep stern watch over the river valley. One Indian wears a feather headdress, the other a wide headband around long hair, both faces formed by the vagaries of wind erosion and crumbling rock. Eerie. Mesmerizing.

Stranger still, Jim tells me about the Marfa lights, those strange clouds of white luminescence appearing frequently and with incomprehensible characteristics upriver on the Texas side. Jim saw a TV documentary where men with walkie-talkies approached a canyon where the lights had appeared. One set of men went down to the canyon floor to get a closer look, but then radioed back that the lights had completely disappeared. They were gone. "What do you mean?" radioed the men still on the canyon rim. "You're right under the lights. We see you *and* the lights. You can reach up and touch them!"

Ahem.

No wonder people around here believe the Rio Grande, too, has its own strange spirit, one it safeguards by means often mysterious. Take the Tree of Death, for example. It was late morning when Jim brought us around a bend and we saw the large salt cedar tree which had fallen directly over the only navigable channel of the river, with barely three feet of clearance below the tree's trunk.

"This," Jim said with a laugh part humor and part real concern, "is the Tree of Death. We've all got to squeeze against the raft bottom and somehow float under that tree."

Just that morning, two other river guides had canoed down to saw off the tree's most threatening branches. The Rio Grande had chosen carefully, for salt cedar wood is so hard the men had to use a hacksaw. Somehow we floated under this stubborn obstruction, with the tree trunk literally brushing against our backs and hair as we crouched low to the raft floor.

Only later, after the subsequent terrifying event in the canyon and our frantic escape, did I think back to this event, this sawing and maiming of the Tree of Death, and wonder if this wasn't the deed, the catalyst, that provoked the river's wrath.

We stop for lunch on the Mexican side, where I set off on a solo hike up a narrow side canyon known for its blue-tinted limestone walls and small vinergaroon scorpions. Two-thousand-year-old pictographs of bison and deer, left by long-forgotten Indians, adorn the canyon's upper reaches.

Back on the river, an enormously tall and broad rock wall looms into view just before sunset, seemingly blocking our way. It's the Mesa de Anguila, a.k.a. the Mesa of Eels, and it's cleaved right down the middle by the towering, doorlike entrance to Santa Elena Canyon. We've arrived.

White-throated swifts dive for insects along the canyon rim as we set up camp on a rocky beach just outside the entrance, dwarfed by the intimidating beauty of five-hundred-foot cliffs which will soar to three times that size inside. Sentinel Butte is still visible in the far distance, the chiseled Indian faces watching us like spies as a violently beautiful sunset lights the cactuses on fire and turns the river purple and makes the sky a slow-exposure eruption of tangerine flames.

Jason, the guide whose raft I've been assigned to tomorrow, tells me over dinner that the only difficult rapids inside the canyon are at a spot ominously called the Rock Slide. Here massive fallen boulders create a bottleneck for rafts. But Jason quickly assures me that the danger of additional falling rocks is absolutely zero. Indeed, neither he nor Jim, with all their experience, has ever seen a single rock fall from a mountainside or canyon into a river. Never. Anywhere. Falling rocks are such a rare and random occurrence that your chances are better of being attacked by a mountain lion.

We sleep that night under the stars, by the murmuring banks of the river. Mexico's proximity affects people's speech down here, so Jim calls our sleeping cushions "taco pads," and someone points up to the constellation Perseus and declares, by God, that he's got a sombrero on his head. And so he does.

The sky is freakishly clear and the stars dense beyond imagining, like ice crystals spread across the universe's window. I lay on my taco pad, with Santa Elena Canyon just feet away, waiting to receive us. I gaze up at the Milky Way galaxy, that long, cloudy band across the sky, mesmerizing to behold, and I sense myself as never before on the outer fringe of that giant cosmic Frisbee, floating on a speck of dust, peering deep into the vast, faraway, unknowable core.

Soon after you enter Santa Elena Canyon the water starts running uphill. You pass through the canyon's monumental rock door, then drift around a sharp bend, then find yourself marvelously entombed by seventy-story-tall limestone cliffs as far as you can see. Then, up ahead, the river starts flowing briskly up a steep incline.

It's an optical illusion, of course. Tectonic forces lifted the stratified bedrock here one hundred million years ago and pushed it up along a fault line. The river then sliced the earth in half, exposing massive rock strata that appear to be perfectly level lines but in fact are tilting downhill in relation to your oncoming raft, making the river appear to flow uphill. Steeply uphill.

This miraculous image, though, competes with others for your attention. For far overhead, mile-long shafts of morning sunlight splash against whole colonies of cliff swallows perched inside delicate clay-pot nests. Below that, peppering the walls, lie unreachable dark caves, offering refuge to wierd rock-climbing cactuses. Farther down still, lie the ancient fossils of clams and oysters and shellfish left by an ancestral sea. And down, down, down— farther down still—lie layers of petrified ash and flowing lava from prehistoric volcanoes.

Then ground zero: the shimmering, shallow Rio Grande, where hand-sized mud turtles, little changed in fifty million years, sun themselves on water-polished boulders. Narrow sand beaches are lush with river cane and seepwillows and the tracks of ringtail cats.

Santa Elena Canyon imprisons you in its beauty. It dominates you utterly the moment you enter. There's no peeking over the tops of those walls at anything else the world has to offer. And climbing out of here is impossible. For the next ten miles you get this world and no other, your raft like a tiny leaf floating through a universe scaled to giants.

A mile into the canyon, we begin to hear the rushing water of the Rock Slide rapids up ahead. Jim, in the lead raft, starts explaining to the other guests how to prepare for this tricky passage. In our raft, Jason turns to me. "We're going to get stuck up there in those rapids," says this twenty-five-year-old with the red beard and ponytail. "There are passages between boulders ahead that are narrower than the rafts. But the raft will give a little if we push and pull and bounce around. We've just gotta work together on this."

I have trouble listening, distracted by the sudden sight of the largest fallen rock I've ever seen, a wedge-shaped monster as big as a three-story building just to our right. There's a proportionally shaped gap up there on the canyon rim where, last week or a million years ago, this rock dislodged itself, fell a thousand feet and, instead of shattering, literally stabbed itself into the bedrock along the river bank. And that's where it rests, a free-standing, trillion-ton stone wedge with a slight tilt.

The sound of crashing water gets louder and the river grows strewn with massive boulders. It's time. We secure our valuables inside steel, twenty-caliber ammunition cans and zip up our life preservers, which look like flack jackets. Jason has a knife strapped to his preserver so he can cut himself free if the raft flips and he gets trapped underneath. I check and recheck my preserver. My mouth is dry.

Sure enough, at the very first rock "slot," where the river gets squeezed between boulders six feet apart, Jim gets stuck. To help him out, Jason decides to row up from behind and give him a bump. But before the rafts touch, the explosion happens.

A gun goes off right behind us.

It shatters our ears—*BANG!*—creating a degree of fright and extreme confusion hard to describe. What in the world? Jason and I instantly turn around to see a splash of water just ten feet behind us, physical proof we're under attack. The splash is at the *exact* spot where our raft had been just five seconds earlier before Jason decided to speed up to bump Jim. My God. How can this be? A bullet almost hit us. Who could be shooting at us? Why?

Reflexively, we crouch low in our raft and Jason begins scanning the canyon rims for a sniper while I yell at Jim: *"Go! Go! Go!"* He's still maddeningly stuck inside the only escape route out of here. Whoever's shooting at us knew we'd be bottled up here; an excellent ambush site. We're sitting ducks.

Jim and the others struggle mightily against the rocks, oars in the boat, using their arms to push and pull against the boulders. Then Jason yells out. *"Rocks! Rocks! Rocks are falling! Watch out!"*

We hit the decks. From high up on the canyon rim, two rocks the size of basketballs are heading directly toward us. Within seconds two more gunshot sounds shatter the canyon air. Just thirty feet behind us, two more splashes send water geysering into the air.

It's a rock slide.

It's coming from the Mexican side.

There is no sniper.

Only later do we understand that the explosions we hear are not coming from the rocks violently slapping against the water surface. The sound is coming from the rocks barreling over one thousand feet down the canyon cliff, entering the Rio Grande, traveling three feet underwater, and then smashing against the rocky river bottom with such explosive force and speed that the column of air behind each rock doesn't have time to close before the sound waves escape upward. Hence, gun blasts.

Never in my life have I been so scared. It takes an eternity for Jim's raft to finally squeeze through the rock slot, all of us cringing through each crawling second, completely certain we'll be crushed at any moment by a shower of more rocks. To me it seems certain that the three ear-piercing blasts so far will, by themselves, trigger more avalanches on both sides.

Finally Jim gets through, then Jason and I pull through with great effort. Then the guides row like men possessed while the rest of us scour the canyon rims for more rocks. We see nothing, but we're far from out of danger. The rafts get stuck again in another boulder pass. Again we struggle free. Then we race down two sets of brisk rapids.

Finally, hearts still sprinting, we realize we're out of trouble. No more rocks have fallen and we're well beyond the initial trouble spot. As the adrenaline rush subsides, it begins to dawn on us what a far-fetched thing has happened. No one will believe us. As if it weren't strange enough that rocks fell at all, almost hitting us, it so happens that only *three* came down. Then no more. Nothing.

It was as if the canyon waited for the perfect moment, took its best shot, missed, then let us pass.

"I don't mind admitting it," Jason said later, resting his arms after all the furious rowing. "That was as scary as anything I've experienced in a long, long, long time."

Later, a guide knowledgeable of the terrain up there on the Mexican side flatly ruled out human involvement. People don't go up there, he said. Ever. Period. It's far too desolate.

So what caused the rocks to fall? The hoof of a wild horse? The echo of our own voices? The removal by wind of that last grain of sand in a one-thousand-year erosion process that finally loosened those cliff-side bruisers?

And why at the *exact* moment we were passing? Over and over again since the day it happened, I've asked myself that question. I mean, what are the chances? Jim and Jason, with all their years on rivers, had never seen a rock fall. Forget almost being *hit* by rocks. They'd never been able to say, "Hey, look. Did you see that rock splash way down there in the distance?" Not once.

So again, what are the chances? Assuming it wasn't the Tree of Death or some other riverine infraction, the only answer seems to be another question.

Amazing Grace in the Texas Desert

What are the chances that wind can carve a sculpture resembling an Indian face? Or that the Marfa Lights happen? Or that life itself exists? Or if life exists, why is it this way? Why a planet with deserts? Why planets around a star? Why stars in galaxies? What are the chances?

Eventually, our necks sore from craning to watch the tops of the walls, we accept that we will not be "attacked" again and the river once more becomes enjoyable. We have lunch, do some climbing, and continue in our rafts. Then, with little warning, Santa Elena Canyon spits us back onto the sprawling desert floor. The tall walls simply end, the vault disappears, and the world has a horizon again. It's like waking abruptly from the deepest possible dream.

I feel blue and confused as we drift away from the gorge, floating toward the takeout point. Why am I not happy and relieved? Only ten feet separated me from certain death back there. Where's the uplifting insight into the preciousness of life? The meaning of it all? Instead my thoughts are vague and uncertain, like the buckling shimmer of a heat mirage. The desert's fighting my memory, my need for a rational conclusion, holding its secrets to the last.

I step off the raft and back onto the desert surface. And, to my surprise, I keep right on floating.

8
Capital Fish Story

I'm standing in a beautiful forest, next to a glimmering stream. I cast my line toward golden-brown pools of cool water full of catfish and bass, perch and carp. My Bosnian guide, Zeljko Koretec, the preeminent expert on this rarely fished stream, is standing one hundred feet upriver, reeling in a two-pound bass. A largemouth.

Zzziiinnngggg! goes his drag as the bass dives again.

All around, I see deer and raccoon tracks. Up and down the creek bank, as far as I can see, there are no other human footprints. No one comes here to fish. It's the ultimate traveler's fantasy. I've given the world the slip, journeyed to a place that is special beyond my imagining.

I took a city bus—the S4—to get here.

A beaver swims past me, five feet away, on his way to a hidden den. My pole bends suddenly. I've hooked another nice catfish. Fifteen inches long. I've stopped counting how many that makes. *Zzziiinnngggg!* goes the drag. I bring him to shore, and when the adrenaline subsides, I hear a distant voice. It floats down a hill, across the creek, through the trees. It pulls me back to Earth:

"Dick! Dick! Did you see the giraffes? They're feeding!"

It's not Africa or Bosnia. It's Rock Creek National Park, deep inside Washington, D.C., a 1,700-acre spread of dense forest running from Maryland to the very edge of downtown, skirting the famous confines of the National Zoo.

"Why does no one fish here?" Zeljko asks. "Your Rock Creek is so wonderful." He's fished here almost every day since emigrating from Bosnia six months earlier. But few Americans bother. Zeljko motions toward the water. There are so many fish we can see them everywhere, quite plainly through the clear water.

"So many fish and no fishermen," Zeljko says. "Why?"

I know the answer and so do you. It's a cliche but true: People don't take full advantage of the treasures in their own hometowns. Most Washingtonians can't remember the last time they lingered over those great paintings in the Capitol rotunda or took a lunchtime stroll through the Smithsonian Air and Space Museum. And even those residents and tourists who do venture into the city to take in a museum or performance don't consider exploring Washington's *natural* treasures. Escaping to nature for most people here means putting as many miles between themselves and the Beltway as quickly as possible. All of which makes D.C.'s ecological wonders some our most ignored national assets, banished to the outer realm of stepchild oblivion.

Which is why, to acquaint myself with Washington in a fresh way, I decided to do what a lot of people do to acquaint themselves with more exotic locales: fish it. Why bother to jet off to Idaho or Montana or Alaska, or even drive out to the Shenandoah Valley, to make contact with nature? Just come to the District of Columbia.

Henry David Thoreau, quintessential nature maven, was right: The world's true wildernesses lie underwater. Rock Creek proved to be quite thick with underwater cruisers amid all those majestic trees. Zeljko will come back here tomorrow and catch twenty-five bass, four of them more than two pounds.

The Potomac, meanwhile, along its lazy course past downtown Washington, is one of *the ten best places in America* to catch largemouth bass, according to the Bass Anglers Sportsman Society. Fishing shows from across the country tape Potomac segments within sight of the Kennedy Center—yet we locals remain oblivious. Washington's Anacostia River, meanwhile, despite some problems, is a very decent river for sport fishing, harboring most of the thirty-two species one can hook within the district lines. And the tidal basin? How about thirty-five-inch striped bass in June after they've come up from the Atlantic to spawn? You want fly-fishing? Try the Constitution Gardens pond, next to the Vietnam Memorial. A microscopic group of fly rod eccentrics says it's "utterly outstanding" for bass and bluegill in the spring.

"In terms of fishing, many of our water resources are definitely underutilized," says Jon Siemien, senior fisheries biologist within the D.C. government's Fisheries and Wildlife Division. (Yes, the city has one of those, too.)

So here's the message for Washingtonians and visitors: Travel inward to the city core. Put yourself at the water's edge and get to know the town in a way you've never expected. The fishing's great—probably better than anything near where you live, with a physical setting that's more tranquilizing than you've ever understood. And with each cast into that watery reflection of the Washington Monument, travel inward to your own core.

That's what fishing, finally, is all about: getting inside yourself, below the surface of things, relaxing, recharging. It's about catching your breath—deep down—while connecting again with living things in a living world.

"When I fish, everything is all right," says Zeljko. "I forget about the war in my country. I forget about my prison time there. I go home from Rock Creek and everything is all right."

Imagine what it can do for a crummy day at the office.

There's only one shop in all of Washington dedicated exclusively to bait and tackle. From my home in nearby Takoma Park, Maryland, I take the Red Line subway train to Union Station, then walk fifteen minutes to G&S Bait & Tackle at 421 Morse Street NE. It's in a warehouse district, across from the Hartman Meat Co., spitting distance from the D.C. Farmers Market.

Forklifts whiz past me as I enter the tiny, 750-square-foot tackle shop. Inside I'm greeted by a chorus of crickets, a forest of fishing rods, and the smell of bait fish. Crab pots dangle overhead.

On Fridays and Saturdays, Shirley Gupton, the smiling, voluble owner, unlocks her door at 3:00 A.M. for the early birds heading down to D.C.'s Hains Point or Buzzard Point on the Potomac or far-off spots in southern Maryland. Other days she opens at a leisurely 5:00 A.M. "Miss Shirley," as her customers call her, tells me there's just enough business in the district to keep her on this side of solvency. She closes down the store in November and reopens in April, working in between as a substitute schoolteacher. A strange combination of professions, I remark.

"Not at all," she says. "I like being around children, and most fishermen are just that: grown-up children. So we get along."

I survey the bait offerings: crickets, minnows, sandworms, mill worms, night crawlers, red wigglers, nuclear worms, dough balls (for carp), clam "snouts," and all manner of floats, crankbait lures, topwater lures, spinners, and plastic worms.

I load up, buying a rod and reel, assorted bait and tackle, and a D.C. fishing license—$5 for residents, $7.50 for nonresidents like myself.

So equipped, I say good-bye to Miss Shirley and hail a cab on Florida Avenue for the National Arboretum. My rod is jutting out the cab's back window as we reach the arboretum entrance. It's a sunny, breezy June Monday and a pleasant walk through the trees takes me—happy fisherman child—to an upper stretch of the Anacostia River. It's my first visit here and, reaching the river, I promptly lapse into a fit of disbelief. This is Washington?

Buffered by the arboretum on one side and more forested parkland on the other, the tableau before me might as well be an isolated, rural finger of the Chesapeake. I sit on the bank and watch two great blue herons stalk fish in a lush stretch of marsh grass. A mallard takes flight, wing tips beating the water, raising staccato splashes. Here and there the river boils with surfacing fish.

I walk the bank, casting spinnerbait. I catch two small white perch over the next two hours, but the tide's going out and the fish really aren't biting, so I just enjoy the scenery. On a subsequent visit, I'm astonished and delighted to see a bald eagle here. D.C. wildlife officials say it's not so uncommon.

And what of the Anacostia's pollution? It's there. The river's much more shallow than the Potomac, and because it's technically not a river but an estuary, the urban pollutants that cross its banks don't flush so well. Also, the majority of the district's surface streets drain into the Anacostia. (Rock Creek, meanwhile, suffers from water temperature problems in the summer when rainwater from steaming hot asphalt streets barrels in. Trout, as a result, cannot live in the creek.)

But the Anacostia is still able to support a rich array of life forms. D.C. biologist Siemien compares the Anacostia to the Chesapeake Bay. It has problems, yes, but it's still a fine fishery and not as polluted as it once was. Still, throughout the district, the city advises against eating captured carp, catfish, and eel, whose flesh is more likely than other species to store toxins. At the moment, I'm thinking striped bass and feeling lazy. I switch to clam as bait, tie a float on my line, cast, prop up my rod, stretch out, and . . . fall asleep.

This is not normal behavior for me. It's my first nap in forever, in fact. Even when I relax, generally, I prefer to worry. I can fuss over all kinds of problems while on a leisurely jog or working in my garden. But here in the district, fishing amid the great blue herons, seeing not a soul all afternoon, hearing the breeze through the trees and only an occasional, very faint police siren, I'm just too relaxed to worry. So I sleep.

I wake an hour later, pleasantly groggy, my bait gone. I reel in and decide to break camp. The afternoon's waning. It's time for some sunset fishing. It's time to head downtown.

◆ ◆ ◆

I'm back on the Red Line subway at rush hour, standing with one hand on a rail, the other holding my tackle box and rod. The train's jammed with the usual mix of wrinkled suits, office dresses, worn-out custodians, discarded newspapers. Every set of eyes has a post-traumatic vacancy—everyone sucked dry by the fangs of another workday.

Except me. I've had a nap. I've been fishing. And people stare at me now. If you have any doubts about the merits of fishing in this city, ride a Metro train with all of your gear. People fix me with expressions of fascination and amusement—looks I've seen only when riding the subway with my infant son or traveling in full costume to a Halloween party. People smile. For them, I think, I'm a reminder that there's another way. Life doesn't have to be like this. Just knowing this, seeing it in the form of my tackle box, seems to make people feel better.

It boils down to goodness, I think. People equate fishing with goodness. If we paid guys to stand in trains at rush hour just holding fishing rods, perhaps crime would go down, divorce would decrease. Perhaps. During my mission to fish the district, my fishing rod will travel all the city's subway lines—Red, Green, Blue, Orange, and Yellow. It will walk through the great hall at Union Station and hail several more cabs and wander down K Street. It will take the S4 bus, the 70, the 54, and the E2.

It will get lots of smiles.

At the Metro Center stop I switch to the Blue Line and get out at Smithsonian station. Soon I'm on the tidal basin, hunting for largemouth and striped bass. It's a glorious summer evening. The wind has died down, the tide's coming in, and conditions are good for fishing. Across the entire basin, I see only one other fisherman, an older man casting near the FDR Memorial. He's just caught a fifteen-inch largemouth. I sidle over.

"A white wiggler," he says, flashing the plastic worm he used before heading off to his car on Independence Avenue. I dig out something similar from my tackle box and, sure enough, I catch a fourteen-inch largemouth, a real pole bender. I happily throw him back.

Capital Fish Story

Next I wander to the Constitution Gardens pond on the other side of the Reflecting Pool. I'm amazed to find a fly fisherman launching curlicues of line through the golden evening light and onto the pond surface.

His name is Brian Cassidy, and he keeps casting as I pepper him with questions. Yes, he's a serious fisherman, he says. He grew up fly-fishing the trout streams of southern Pennsylvania, and he comes to this concrete-edged pond with all the camera-toting tourists and noisy ducks and the Washington Monument within view because the fishing is "absolutely great." He regularly hooks two-pound bass, and on a good night he'll catch four or five really nice ones in ninety minutes.

"My friends outside of D.C. wouldn't believe it," he says. He is wearing sunglasses and a rugby shirt. "They think all that happens in D.C. is shootings. They wouldn't believe the fly-fishing's this good right here."

In five years of fishing regularly at the Constitution Gardens pond, he's seen maybe two or three other fly-fishermen. "It's almost like my personal, private pond," he says. He gets best results between April and June from 6:00 P.M. to sunset. The largemouth bass respond well to small flies and larger hair flies, he says, and the catfish sometimes hit streamers.

Cassidy, who lives in the district, says he fishes mostly to blow off steam from his high-stress pharmaceutical job in Vienna. The goal is to stop thinking completely, he says. "I try not to make decisions or solve problems here. I just want something stupid. Just catch fish."

Cassidy keeps casting, and for a while neither of us says anything in the beautiful sunset light. In the middle of a town famous for loudmouths touting new ideas, we remain absolutely silent, putting the brakes on all thoughts. We don't enter our breathing. We enter the rhythm of his casting.

Same results.

It's 6:20 A.M. and I'm directly in the landing path of a Boeing 757 at D.C.'s Reagan National Airport. Bill Kramer, my professional bass guide for the day, has launched his twenty-foot bass boat at Gravelly Point Park, just off the George Washington Parkway, next to the main hangars for US Airways. But to get from the boat ramp to the main body of the Potomac, you have to float directly under the running lights—mounted on pilings—just off the northern tip of Reagan National's main runway. It's a memorable experience seeing landing gear and wing rivets in such detail so early in the morning. And who needs coffee with all the skull-rattling noise? But if you're fishing the D.C. Potomac, you launch where you can—and within minutes we're out in the river, away from the noise, happily casting into a bed of coontail milfoil grass on a sand bed upriver from the Woodrow Wilson Bridge.

Kramer, thirty-nine, a former concert sound engineer for Judas Priest and Ted Nugent, is arguably the crown prince of Potomac fishing. He's won more than eighty tournaments on the river, earning big cash prizes, boats, even a Chevy pickup. His biggest catch was a 9.2-pound largemouth in Smoot Cove just below the Wilson Bridge on the Maryland side.

And sure enough, this morning, Kramer's the first to catch a fish, a fifteen-inch largemouth using a tandem willow white spinner pulled through a thick bed of grass. We move later to the Washington Channel, where, along the bulkheading of Fort McNair, across from the columned mansions of the army brass, I hook a bass of similar size using a quarter-ounce rattletrap in chrome and blue.

It's a cloudy, gray, almost foggy morning that's beautiful in a lonely way, despite the urban landscape all around. Today we'll cast within sight of the Lincoln Memorial, the *USA Today* building, the Pepco plant in Alexandria, and the Georgetown University bell tower. All the while, osprey and geese will wing past us, and red-eared slider turtles will bob to the surface, eyeing us blankly.

Kramer, who calls fishing his "religion," began guiding ten years ago so he could spend more time on the water. He gestures through the misty, eerie air, past an osprey nest perched atop a channel marker, toward the forested Theodore Roosevelt Island in the distance. "This world," he says, "is not like the rest of the world we live in."

Indeed it isn't. Touring bass pros regularly rank the tidal Potomac, from the district on down to the Chesapeake, as one of the best fisheries for large-mouths in America. Fisheries biologists, meanwhile, rave about the river's extraordinary variety of species, from bass to bluefish to sawtooth walleyes to American shad. Population densities are also very high.

D.C. officials sometimes see schools of a thousand perch during electro-fishing surveys. The Potomac's relatively pollution-free flow down from Appalachia—combined with the nutrient-rich character of tidal environments and the wide range of fish species coming up from the Chesapeake and Atlantic—accounts largely for this abundant environment.

So why do so few people in the D.C. area come here for fishing trips, or even know enough to consider it? I asked Kramer. "Because in the nineteen-fifties and sixties the Potomac was a flowing cesspool," he says. "It was a disgrace, it was so polluted. If you fell in the river, it was recommended you go to the hospital for examination. Now the river's much better. Pollution controls are higher and the fish populations are mostly solid.

"But people still think of it as the old river. So people don't understand how good the fishing is here."

Improvements to the district's Blue Plains water treatment plant, just below Bolling Air Force Base, have contributed most to the river's recovery, Kramer says. It is along the wooden dock of this very same plant that Kramer catches the biggest fish of our outing: a 4.5-pound largemouth hooked on a jig and pig. It's a real bruiser.

Together we catch and release a respectable share of bass for the day, stopping at a dozen different spots. We fish more grass beds up and down the river. We go back to Reagan National to fish the runway-light pilings. We fish for smallmouth bass under the Yellow Line subway bridge, casting and reeling as passengers zip past overhead.

Too soon, it's time to quit. We pass the Kennedy Center, Kramer dodging driftwood with one hand on the wheel and checking his voice mail by cell phone with the other hand. The world is taking us back.

Surprisingly, of all my D.C. fishing trips, it is on the Potomac, with the city in full view all around, that I feel farthest away from the town I know. It's my first time actually out on the river, in a boat, and the city's landmarks present themselves from unfamiliar new angles. Framed only by the Potomac, the Lincoln Memorial looks like a whole new work of art, as do many of Washington's treasures. It's the visual equivalent of what's already been happening inside my head. Coming into town and getting on the water has transported me far away—again.

Two other moments stick out in my mind from my angling tour of Washington.

One evening, I'm fishing for striped bass near Fletcher's Boathouse, just down from the Chain Bridge on a forested bank of the Potomac. Near sunset, two Cambodian men appear from the trees carrying large cast nets. Fifty feet upstream from me, they launch their nets with utter delicacy, and I watch as the circular nets float dreamlike through the air, falling evenly toward the river, then softly shattering the surface. Then comes the quick, hand-over-hand reeling in of the lines, and another cast. It's a sight I've not seen since traveling through Vietnam's Ha Long Bay years before.

The other episode involves fishing the Anacostia River with Sonny Mickens, a silver-bearded, sixty-two-year-old retiree I meet at G&S Bait & Tackle one morning. He takes me to his favorite fishing spot just up from the Eleventh Street Bridge, next to the Washington Yacht Club. It's simultaneously one of the ugliest and most beautiful places I've fished in the district. Weeds climb unchecked all around a broken-down picnic table, and trash is scattered liberally about the riverbank.

But there's an odd serenity to this shady little spot, a feeling amplified by the group of extremely friendly and funny homeless winos who appear to live here. They offer me a rusting, secondhand lawn chair and return to their own fishing. They use discarded line and hooks, combined with plastic soda bottles for floats and worms for bait dug up by the nearby train track. Quite drunk, they throw the whole mess into the water by hand, using no poles. And they catch fish. Indeed, Mickens says this is one of the best places he knows for catfish. He once caught a catfish here "as long as the dashboard of a car." The tradition is to give everything you catch to the indigent hosts, who earn their keep by keeping you laughing with their nutty stories. D.C. cops regularly drop by, not to hassle the winos or anyone else, but to relax on their breaks at this out-of-the-way spot not far from the navy yard. One motorcycle cop named Jesse smokes a pipe on the bank next to me as Mickens and I keep fishing and talking.

Mickens says he's been fishing in the district all of his life, from trips to Buzzard Point as a child (his family salted the fish down in a barrel behind their home) to his current afternoons fishing in retirement.

"It improves your outlook," he says. "Down here on the river, there's nothing to get upset about. Your outlook stays low-key and positive."

He casts again, then motions in the direction of the U.S. Capitol, twenty blocks directly behind us on the other side of the train track. "Maybe if these congressmen and other leaders would just get out and fish more, maybe every day even, they'd have that peace of mind I got, and maybe we'd have better laws. I mean, the water's right here, all around them. What are they waitin' for? Just go fish."

III

In the Mountains
of Heaven

9

Going Manhole Crazy in Kyrgyzstan

Why are all the manhole covers in Bishkek, Kyrgyzstan, disappearing? Where, exactly, are they going? I walk through this former Soviet city, now the capital of a newly independent Central Asian nation of 4.5 million people, and one of the first things I notice are the dangerously uncovered manholes on almost every block. What's going on here, anyway?

My friend Galina, a Russian journalist, was stepping out of a taxi last year when she disappeared down one of the manholes, swallowed alive. She dropped several feet and broke her leg in three places. I nearly do the same each time I go jogging. I move through streets of drab Soviet architecture, bingeing on poured concrete, wanting very much to look up at the enormous, heart-stopping mountains edging the city. The mountains are capped with snow so bright it makes you blink, part of the Tian Shan range, the Mountains of Heaven. Up there is a world of wild yaks, snow leopards, and twenty-thousand-foot peaks. But I rarely look up while I jog. A bruised heel from a recent near miss with an open manhole discourages me. I glare at the sidewalk.

The manhole covers disappear in parking lots, on sidewalks, on roads. I saw an old Soviet Lada blocking a main street one evening, its front tire half buried in a manhole, axle broken. Careless cyclists are propelled into midair. We're talking hundreds, maybe thousands, of covers. Yet how many possibilities are there? The covers are too awkward and useless to steal. Too big and heavy to misplace. It's a mystery in a country full of mysteries.

When I wrote a friend announcing I was moving to Kyrgyzstan (my wife had taken a job there as a Peace Corps administrator), he wrote back saying the country's name looked like a typo, like when your fingers wander from the home keys for half a line. "I hope it doesn't *feel* like a typo when you get there," he said.

Actually, most days, it does. Bordering western China, just a stone's throw north of Afghanistan, Kyrgyzstan is a country coming and going, rising and falling—but mostly falling. Against the backdrop of sparkling mountains, where Kyrgyz shepherds still live in ancient-style yurts as they mind summer flocks, construction cranes rust away in downtown Bishkek, idled by the post-Soviet economic free fall. The doors to the golden West have been unlocked and flung wide open, to be sure, which means you can now find Peanut M&Ms and Snickers bars mixed in with the cabbage and beets of streetside markets. You can even buy Barf dishwashing liquid—now *there's* a typo—imported from the Islamic Republic of Iran.

But few people can afford any of this. Factories are closing. Unemployment is rising. Skilled labor is fleeing. A poverty boom is in full swing. The new government, still trying to get its sea legs, is as busted as anyone. Pension payments are dwindling to nothing and school teachers are paid regularly with bags of flour and bottles of vodka. There's not even enough money for a good run of Lenincide, a requisite sport in most ex-Soviet republics. Lenin's fifty-foot-tall statue still towers above central Bishkek, a hulk of concrete and gaudy earnestness, gesturing in a strange, idiotic way toward the mountains. One plan is to saw him off at his huge ankles, tip him over, and pick up the boulder-sized pieces. But the government doesn't have the money to do it.

While Lenin is present and accounted for, the manhole covers most certainly are not. I recently resolved to crack the mystery by approaching my friend Marat, a Kyrgyz shepherd. In a country where sheep outnumber people five to one, flocks are nearly as common as air even in the capital. Marat grazes his sheep around my apartment building in downtown Bishkek several days a week.

Before independence in 1991, Bishkek was a city peopled predominately with Russian settlers, colonists on the outer fringe of the Soviet empire. By the time I moved there in 1995, the Russians were emigrating in droves back to the motherland, fleeing the pinch of minority status, taking with them scarce skills and higher education levels. Meanwhile, the traditionally nomadic Kyrgyz like Marat, with their gentle-spirited manners and Oriental features, were coming down from their highland haunts, down from the Mountains of Heaven, trailed by their flocks of organic lawn mowers. The Kyrgyz now hunt scarce jobs and decent housing amid the alluring lights of the valley-bottom city. And like everyone, they learn to sidestep the open manholes.

"I haven't lived here long enough to know the answer," Marat said when I asked him where all the missing manhole covers go. He said he tried his best to keep his flocks from getting too close to the holes, but beyond that he didn't give the issue much thought. I watched as he downed another afternoon cup of fermented mare's milk, a sort of national drink among the Kyrgyz. He looked relaxed, imperturbable. He laughed in a friendly way at my curious manhole inquiry. "Ask the merchants at the market," he said. "Maybe they know the answer. I'm just a man with a few sheep."

I left Marat to his flock and headed to the Market of a 1000 Things in central Bishkek. There I found Talgat Rafikov, a laid-off Tartar factory worker, selling random household goods spread across a ragged sheet of sidewalk plastic. The ancient Silk Road once passed through this part of Kyrgyzstan with its fabled traffic of spices and carpets, silk and gold. Rafikov's fare was markedly less seductive. One steel fork, a pair of old scissors, some electrical wires, a rusting plumber's wrench—all taken from his own home.

"Of course I know where the manhole covers go," Rafikov said when I asked. "Like everything else, they break sooner or later. A truck runs over one and it breaks into pieces and falls into the hole. But the factory that makes new covers is closed down now. All the factories are closing. Thirty years I worked as a factory welder. Now I have no job, and this new government— ha!—it gives me nothing. I haven't had a piece of bread in three days, God as my witness. I have to sell little things from my house just to have bread."

He continued. "In the Soviet time, we had manhole covers and we had bread. And if you fell down a manhole without a cover, you could go to the government and someone would be in trouble. But now. Ha! We're doomed!"

I asked him the obvious question. "Would you prefer to have the Soviet Union back?"

The pause that followed seemed unusually long for a hungry man.

"Yes," he said. "I mean, no. I mean, yes. If we could have the Union back, but with more openness and freedom than before, then it would be okay. But otherwise, I guess no."

Another interesting response for a hungry man.

I walked a few blocks thinking about Rafikov's manhole theory, passing a few open holes in the process. I decided to ask Cholpon, a Kyrgyz businesswoman I knew, what she thought. Cholpon runs a small sidewalk eatery from a yurt along a main Bishkek street within view of old Lenin Square, the mountains, and the concrete statue of Lenin himself looking nearly as tall as the peaks. Cholpon got her yurt as a gift from her father. Her father got it when his cooperative farm disbanded and the property was divvied up. He gave it to Cholpon to start her restaurant.

I ordered a bowl of Chinese noodles inside the wool yurt, where brightly patterned Kyrgyz *shyrdak* carpets, sewn with camel-hair thread, lined the floor and walls.

Going Manhole Crazy in Kyrgyzstan

"Actually, I don't know where they go," Cholpon said of the manhole covers as she arrived with my noodles. I told her of Rafikov's theory. "Hmmm," she said. "That sounds right to me. The factory *is* closed. When the covers break—that's it."

She tended to other customers, then returned. Business wasn't bad, she said. She liked having her own little restaurant. This would have been criminal behavior under the Soviets. She would have been thrown in jail for serving noodles this way. Now, Cholpon said, she mostly likes her new country, except for the protection money she has to pay the growing local mafia. Upon request, she'll prepare for you the supreme Kyrgyz delicacy: boiled sheep's head served whole with the eyeballs lightly seasoned. Cholpon's name means "brightest star in the sky."

Over the next few days, I peered down several open manholes, failing to find evidence of a single broken cover, and so doubting Rafikov's theory. I did find a soiled mattress down one hole where someone was obviously passing nights. A viral outbreak of Manhattan-style homelessness was apparently creeping in with the Snickers and Peanut M&Ms.

A Peace Corps volunteer in Bishkek, out of the blue, offered new evidence in the manhole mystery. He happened upon a makeshift gymnasium one day where Russian bodybuilders were firming up with huge manhole covers symmetrically affixed to either end of long weightlifting bars. The men, quite literally, were pumping iron. Streetwise fitness.

Unfortunately, there aren't enough weightlifters in all of Bishkek to account for more than a handful of manhole covers, leaving the question of where the rest are going. The hunt for an answer finally began to warm up as I was cycling through a Bishkek park with my American friend Dan, a local history buff. With an air of sadness, Dan pointed to a blank patch of grass in the park.

"There used to be a huge bust of Yuri Gagarin right there," he said. "You know, the Soviet cosmonaut who was the first man to orbit the earth. But a year ago, Yuri just disappeared. Poof. People came to the park one day and he was gone."

Dan didn't seem to think post-independence animosity toward Russians had any part in it. Unlike the Armenians, Latvians, and numerous other nationalities now freed from the Russian yoke, the Kyrgyz hold few grudges. Maybe it's the clean mountain living. They shrug in a cheerful way as if to say, "That's all over now. Why cry over spilled mare's milk? *Nyet problem.*"

Dan had a different explanation for the missing bust. He pointed to the host of still-standing stone sculptures in the park while mentioning that Yuri Gargarin had been made of something much more precious: bronze. "I think Yuri got stolen," Dan said. "He was ripped off."

Before going on, it's worth noting the great extent of that loss. As Dan described it, the bronze bust was quite impressive, very large, with Yuri's intricate space helmet cast in high-tech detail all around his brave Russian face. The bust was one of the last local reminders that this region, "Kirghizia" under the Soviets, was until recently part of a country that sent men in spaceships up to the heavens. Frankly, I'd never have believed it otherwise, not after seeing what happens when my Russian and Kyrgyz friends visit my apartment. They ogle the CD player and telephone answering machine, to be sure. But what impresses them most is the simple, manual can opener lying on the kitchen counter. My friends have never seen such a tool. They laugh in startled amazement as it's put to use, easily liberating a supply of olives or tuna. All their lives they've used knives to open cans, poking and tearing at the tin, and, not infrequently, their own hands. The same U.S.S.R. that put men into outer space didn't mass produce the simplest household tool. "Space was more important than people," said one Russian acquaintance, with heartbreaking candor, of the old system.

My friend Mike, an economic officer at the U.S. embassy in Bishkek, confirmed Dan's suspicion of a sculpture heist. "Yuri was definitely stolen," Mike said of the bronze park bust. "No question about it. He probably wound up in China. That's where all your manhole covers are going, too. Little by little. They're smuggled out of the country and sold in Kashgar (a city in western China) and melted down as scrap metal. It's economics."

Going Manhole Crazy in Kyrgyzstan

So thievery was at the root of the manhole matter, after all. Mystery solved. Simple economics. Or so Mike claimed. I'll admit I was at first quite skeptical. Mike was one of the sharpest foreign-service wonks I'd ever met, but he worked at the wackiest, most unconventional U.S. embassy one could possibly imagine, a sort of typo embassy. This new postage-stamp country, wrinkled end-to-end with daunting mountains, was really out there, the mother of all backwaters, the last call on the State Department's hardship train into the lost heart of newly opened Central Asia.

It showed in the embassy's absurdly tiny building in Bishkek, with its corrugated asbestos roof and log walls and pet "watch rooster" out front strutting around in noisy security patrols. Inside, conditions were so cramped that the top-secret communications room was pressed right up against the embassy bathroom, meaning you overheard confidential calls to Washington while you relieved yourself, and the State Department operatives in downtown D.C. heard toilets flushing half a world away. Such are the quirks of far-flung, backwoods diplomacy. It's a good thing you can't hear marijuana growing, I suppose, because it flourishes in Kyrgyzstan, a native weed, popping up all over Bishkek, including—somewhat to the embassy's embarrassment—in the park right outside the U.S. compound. By late summer it gets chest-high in places.

I finally balked at Mike's manhole comments. Wasn't it a little far-fetched to label the covers booty? Wasn't it sort of social suicide creating all those booby traps able to fell the thief and his family as easily as anyone else? You might as well steal the brakes from all the city's cars or poison the water supply.

"Yes it's crazy," Mike said. "But that's where the economy is right now. It's that desperate." Local banks were teetering toward failure left and right, he added. Per capita annual income was down a third to $300 since 1991. "Scavenging scrap metal is starting to look better and better. Even manhole covers."

Mike mentioned that he'd recently been invited to one Kyrgyz city for the grand opening of a new trolley-bus system. But right before the mayor threw the switch, the ceremony was abruptly canceled and all the VIPs sent home: Someone had stolen tons of crucial copper wiring from the trolley system just the night before.

As it turned out, the assortment of purloined metal went by mule and by car to western China, scraps under wraps, off to an ironically booming Communist economy free of the doldrums of newly capitalist Kyrgyzstan. The Chinese government didn't exactly show its gratitude for this new source of cheap I-beams. Every so often it still tested nuclear bombs near its western border, patiently waiting till prevailing winds blew toward Kyrgyzstan, according to the Bishkek papers. For a long and surreal week after each explosion, tens of thousands of people in Kyrgyzstan walked around with slurred speech and wobbly legs—not from the alleged fallout, but the huge doses of vodka widely believed to protect one against it.

So I had my answer. The manhole covers were being hijacked. End of story. Good old-fashioned thievery. And nothing, it seemed, could be done about it. Or could it? I had begun to notice something interesting on Bishkek's streets: a few long-uncovered manholes were suddenly and inexplicably regaining their lids. They were actually being fixed. The city obviously still had a small stash of replacement covers. I decided to make like a squeaky wheel and, for my own safety, report the covers closest to my apartment stolen and in need of replacement.

Stepping into the marble overkill of Bishkek's city hall was, it turned out, like stepping into a diorama of old Soviet party life. A guard with a holdover hammer-and-sickle badge led me down a hall lined with socialist worker art and full of the sounds of manual typewriters, riffling forms, and official stamps lowered with resounding authority. I met with Ishembi, a man who described himself as "assistant to the assistant of the first deputy chair of the mayor's committee on infrastructure." He took my name, number, and the location of the problem manholes. He assured me that both the mayor and the president of the republic had decreed the manhole situation a national priority.

Going Manhole Crazy in Kyrgyzstan

"So new covers *are* available?" I said hopefully. "There's still a factory pro-ducing them here?"

"I'm sorry," Ishembi said with stiffness, "but I'm not at liberty to answer those questions. I can only say that we will do our best."

For most of the time I was in Ishembi's small, bare office, his phone rang and rang and rang while he pretended not to hear a thing.

I walked out of the meeting telling Elmira, my interpreter, that little seemed to have changed from the old, stultifying days of Soviet red tape. She laughed, saying I couldn't be more wrong. Under the Soviets, a huge amount of money went into the bureaucracy and a tiny trickle of services came out. Now, with independence, a tiny trickle of money goes in and *nothing* comes out. She wasn't optimistic Ishembi would ever call.

Leaving city hall, it occurred to me that a perfectly appropriate international development project for Kyrgyzstan might involve helping city governments re-cover and perhaps even lock their manholes. UNICEF was working here to stem a diphtheria epidemic in the countryside, a disease usually associated with poorest Africa. But what about the endemic manhole situation? It was surely a public health threat on a par with a minor disease. Yet not a dime of foreign assistance money was being earmarked for the cause, in part because most of the "aid" organizations—the U.S. Agency for International Develop-ment, the European Community, Germany's GTZ—were too busy "privatiz-ing" and "restructuring" the old Communist-run banks and factories (read closing them down) to worry about much of anything else.

Bishkek, in fact, was crawling with economic consultants of every conceivable stripe and Western origin—Austrians, Brits, Yanks, New Zealanders. Many of them openly groused what a pity it was so many of the skilled-labor Russians had emigrated, leaving behind the allegedly less capable Kyrgyz who couldn't quite connect the dots when it came to the simplest economic concepts. Never mind the sudden evaporation of Soviet sponsorship and the corresponding lack of any real investment capital, natural resources, or modern commercial traditions. Everything seemed to boil down to one basic point in aid workers' eyes: The Kyrgyz were impossible hillbillies. They wouldn't listen. They were a tad shiftless to boot. The consultants' elaborate chalkboard schemes calling for a national "stock exchange" and "joint-venture commodity enhancement" projects were, in fact, perfectly sound. The natives just kept getting in the way.

Despite these setbacks, the Western experts managed to survive in good form in this mountain capital. USAID, for example, had shipped in a fat pack of Price Waterhouse wunderkinds to do much of its privatization dirty work. Most of the PW hired guns were in their twenties, couldn't speak Russian or Kyrgyz, made as much as $50,000 a year tax free, got a housing allowance, *and* pulled down a nice per diem. They liked to go helicopter skiing on weekends.

In a couple of years, of course, virtually all of this "assistance" money will disappear like snowmelt rushing down a mountain holler. The consultants will go home then, having given Kyrgyzstan all the help it can possibly stand, having privatized and restructured the country right out of the Second World and into the Third, completing the West's historic rescue of Soviet Central Asia.

But at least I had my answer. My quest was over. I saw my friend Galina, the one who broke her leg falling into a manhole, and told her I'd uncovered the thriving black market in manhole covers. I told her about my trip to city hall, too. Then I listened as she unraveled my work.

"Don't hold your breath," she said. "The city's *not* the one replacing those manhole tops you've seen on the street. Look at the covers closely. They're not new. They're old and scratched up. Why is that?"

She was right, actually. The covers *were* aged and rather beat-up. After my long search, Galina was exploding the scrap-metal theory as a blanket explanation. She didn't doubt that many of the missing covers were being spirited to China for cash. Times were definitely hard enough for that. But it was also the case that Bishkek residents sometimes make good the dangerous loss of covers on their streets by secretly stealing replacement covers from the next block. It was, in short, a sort of Darwinian scramble: People guarded their own street by worsening their neighbors', setting off a bizarre, citywide chain

reaction of manhole musical chairs. That's why I'd seen manholes with replaced covers, Galina said. It had nothing to do with the government.

My last hope of city help dissolved with the news of this ongoing re-
arrangement of streetside booby traps. It was, quite simply, a crowning absurdity in a system best expressed by the round cover I saw one day forcibly
inserted—literally stomped down—atop a square manhole.

It's perhaps an even greater absurdity in a place like this to pull out the crystal ball and try to divine the future. Who's got time to think about tomorrow
when, like me on my evening jogs, everyone's wholly focused on where their
foot's falling *right now?* As a nation, it's Kyrgyzstan's unfortunate lot that no
new direction now presents itself free of that same constant fear of falling.

One thing, at least, is certain: The future won't look anything like the past.
Scrap-metal attrition to China will eventually end the manhole shuffle for
lack of parts. Finite patience and budgets will send the last privatizing West-
erners home. More hard times will expel many, if not most, of the remaining
Russians. Only then, perhaps, will all the con games finally come to an end,
all the useless efforts, made over and over again, on almost every level, of trying to get something out of nothing in this isolated mountain remove.

Meanwhile, the Kyrgyz shepherds, with their endless flocks of sheep, aren't
going anywhere. The future, whatever it brings, lies with these mountain people. Told to be silent for so many years, they just haven't quite found a voice with
which to articulate their deepest national values and aspirations. They'll continue to drift down from the Mountains of Heaven, sidestepping the open
manholes, wondering where all the funny visitors went, their sheep eating the
grass growing up through cracks in Lenin Square. Lenin himself will doubtless
hang around a while longer, worth less than scrap metal and so allowed to stand
unmolested, a reminder if nothing else of the sheer weight of past years. But
eventually he'll fall too, shattering into boulder-sized pieces, and something
new cannot help but rise in his absence—finally and steadily—up from the
weeds and rubble.

10
silk Road shepherds

It is a shock, of course, to learn that my guide can exit his body and assume the shape of a tree. He makes this claim as we are tossing back cup after cup of fermented mare's milk while sitting outside a yurt surrounded by a meadow of purple daisies. Behind us soar snow-laden peaks, tall and lithely beautiful, shaping the very heart of Kyrgyzstan's fabled Mountains of Heaven.

My guide, whose name is Ishen, gestures across the meadow. "I can become that fir tree over there," he says, "and view the world entirely the way that tree does." He can also become an ant crawling along the ground, he says. Or a smooth stone at the bottom of a river, gazing up through the cold, rushing water at the mountain sky.

Ishen, in his mid-thirties, has long hair and vaguely Mongolian features. That he is turning out to be a mystic of sorts is just one more surprise I encounter in the mysterious upper altitudes of this obscure corner of the former Soviet Union. Weary of the societal dysfunctions and bleak concrete of the capital city, Bishkek, I have struck out for the rural, rugged mountains that dominate this nation and constitute the area least touched by the deforming hands of Lenin, Stalin, and their heirs.

For several days now, Ishen's horses have been carrying us through a land few foreigners have ever seen. Hermetically sealed for decades courtesy of Soviet border paranoia, the region cradles a landscape of rare Marco Polo sheep, awesome mountain glaciers glistening at twenty thousand feet, and the ancient customs of semi-nomadic Kyrgyz shepherds.

I am particularly interested in the latter, and Ishen is my conduit to them. There are no roads where we travel, just mountain trails winding up and over narrow passes. We descend into valleys of heart-stopping greenery streaked with roaring snowmelt rivers. We pitch our tents each night next to a different camp of welcoming shepherds, feasting with them atop shyrdak carpets, drinking mare's milk, and sharing stories in the orange flicker of kerosene lamps.

It is enough that these scattered mountain tribes, largely ignored by time, dine on sheep's eyeballs and cure altitude sickness by bathing in the smoke of juniper branches. But before this trip is over, Ishen will carry things further, changing my life in a small way by working a bit of honest-to-goodness . . . well . . . um . . . magic.

There, I said it.

For centuries, Kyrgyz shepherds have broken winter quarters in lowland valleys and headed for the rich summer meadows of the Tian Shan range edging western China. Roughly a fifth of the Kyrgyz people still make the annual trip today, herding cattle and flocks of sheep by horseback into a dream world of thin air and no fences. My search for a guide turned up Ishen Obolbekov, himself the son of traditional shepherds. My friend Phil, an American artist, has joined me, and together we constitute Ishen's very first customers on this trek through an unexplored land.

We all meet in Bishkek, where a wheezing Soviet-made bus takes us east to Ishen's village of Barskoon, five hours away on shimmering Lake Issyk-Kul. Along the way, Ishen says very little. I, meanwhile, can't stop staring at him. He is the only Kyrgyz man I've met with hair flowing down to his shoulders. His face has a brooding, almost Native American look, inviting yet inscrutable, with eyes implying something very deep. He later tells me he is the grandson of a traditional healer. His father hunts with falcons and cures illnesses with long fasts that purify body and soul. Ishen's son is named Tinstyck, the Kyrgyz word for peace.

In Barskoon the next morning, we eat dried apricots to combat altitude sickness—we're starting at around five thousand feet and will go as high as thirteen thousand. Then we set off for the Tian Shan foothills on horseback, toting our gear in traditional woolen Kyrgyz saddlebags. The goal is to circumnavigate an entire range of fairy-tale peaks in six days, covering 130 miles. Joining our party are Ishen's brother Rosh (the expedition cook) and Ishen's dog, a German shepherd named Dingo.

Early into the steady, switchbacking climb into the mountains, I grow awed by the monumental scale of things—huge peaks, titanic sky, colossal shadows. Rivers rush past us, crashing over boulders. A Eurasian sparrowhawk circles overhead, a distant glacier gleams in the sun, a meadow of wild strawberries spreads out below us.

Soon something odd happens. A shepherd, our first, spots us from a distance and spurs his horse toward us. After a gentle-spirited greeting using the Muslim *salaam aleykum* (peace be with you), the shepherd looks at Ishen while gesturing toward Phil and me. "What are they looking for?" he asks.

Ishen laughs. "Nothing," he says. "These men are just travelers. They just want to see the mountains." Ishen translates the shepherd's Kyrgyz into English for us.

The shepherd doesn't believe this. "What are they looking for?" he asks again. "Gold? Horses? Wives? No one has ever come to these mountains for no reason at all."

Ishen repeats his answer, followed by a smiling farewell. We move on, but the question follows us throughout this trip like a peculiar shadow: "What are they looking for?"

We come upon the remains of an ancient Silk Road fort built by Chinese merchants. For centuries, one branch of the famous spice route brought caravans of Bactrian camels through this narrow valley headed west. Yet like so many jewels of this isolated ex-Soviet region, there are no markers heralding the clay fort's historical wonder, leaving us to feel like its discoverers. Ditto for the ancient Tibetan petroglyphs—hawks, wild goats—we find just beyond the fort.

After lunch, Ishen decides we should bolster our acclimatization by climbing—sans horses—to a waterfall one thousand feet up a stout mountainside. By the time Phil and I reach the top, heaving and blowing, Ishen is already there, at the waterfall's edge, gesturing down to the gorgeous tumult of falling water. "Drink a handful of this," Ishen says, "and we Kyrgyz believe you will gain ten more years of life." We follow his example, quaffing the sparkling cold elixir, while Ishen beams with delight at having shared a gift decade with us.

Shuffling back down to my horse, I feel a strange sensation grow inside me. It isn't the water. I don't believe the legend. But I've traveled the world, and this trip is starting to feel different. Ishen seems to be taking us somewhere we hadn't quite reckoned on going. When the next shepherd rides up and asks, "What are these men looking for?" Ishen shrugs and turns to me as if to say, "Well? What should I tell them?"

We make camp that night with an old widow shepherd and her daughters, all wearing brilliantly colored Kyrgyz scarves. The cows around this camp are so fat and happy from the rich mountain grass that they actually try to cajole our dog Dingo into a game of tag of sorts. I never would have believed cows could funhouse in such a preposterous way had I not seen it myself. That night, after a meal of mutton stew, Ishen and I lie on our backs in the grass and watch from nine thousand feet as a downpour of shooting stars festoons the Central Asian sky.

At the start of our trip, Ishen had given Phil and me just one explicit instruction: "Don't lose the whip for your horse," he said. "It's very bad luck in these mountains to lose your whip."

"Right," we said, gripping our whip handles a bit tighter. "Don't lose them. Got it."

The rest of our mountain education comes simply by watching Ishen. We watch how he maneuvers his horse skillfully through violently swollen rivers, how he gives sweets to the children in isolated camps, how he takes off his boots before entering a shepherd's tent. "What are they looking for?" each shepherd asks Ishen, on cue, as we enter.

After a few days, Ishen explains how he can metamorphose into things strewn across the landscape. Through a self-styled meditation, his whole being can leave his body and enter the other object—rock, cloud, tree. It is his way of seeing more of the world, he says, of gaining knowledge of how things fit together. Later, rocking on my horse, I try the technique myself without success. I don't entirely reject the possibility that Ishen can do this, however. In a rugged, shut-off society like this, free from Western logic, one perhaps *could* find less pedestrian ways to move through the world.

We push on, immersed in Kyrgyz culture at every turn. Shepherds show us how to prepare mare's milk, their summer staple. A shepherd pulls a suckling foal away from its mother just as the milk emerges, then milks the mare not unlike a cow. A day of fermentation in a hand-carved wooden barrel gives the drink a tart, smoky, pleasant taste.

These summer months are the happiest time of year for the Kyrgyz. The high-altitude weather, bursting with sunshine, is springlike in feel, adding to the sense of renewal and well-being permeating the lush meadow valleys. A similar feeling prevails in the camps where, passing through, we regularly find a heart-melting youth riot of fertility—foals, calves, kittens, puppies, baby goats, lambs and, somewhere, inevitably, a bundled-up Kyrgyz baby blissfully working at a mother's breast.

A scare comes midweek when Phil does the unthinkable: He loses his whip. We turn our camp upside down to avoid the bad luck that supposedly will follow. At last Phil notices the whip lying in the grass where he was napping earlier.

We begin an ascent toward the highest pass of the trip, thirteen-thousand-foot Howling Pass. The going is steep, and Ishen keeps reminding us to be kind to our horses, letting them switchback as much as they want, easing their terrible task. It is colder up here, the wind stronger, life a bit harder for the shepherds. Ishen is particularly generous giving out candy to children at this altitude, their cheeks burned dark red by wind and sun.

It's embarrassing to admit, but Phil and I begin fighting on this trip. It's perhaps not the best mix of temperaments, putting an artist and a writer in the same small tent for a week. When I shoot photos one day without film in my camera, I somehow blame it on Phil. When he discovers he's brought insufficient pencil lead for sketching, he turns cranky, especially toward me. We even fight over whose horse should carry our tent. It's all quite ridiculous.

Ishen can't help but see all this, though he says nothing—at least not directly. We later come to a valley featuring a particularly old and interesting yurt, and Ishen explains the tent's ingenious design. Round, made of felt and sewn together with camel-hair thread, the Kyrgyz yurt is made for the migrating life. It can be taken down in just one hour by one person and placed entirely atop one horse, Ishen tells us. It takes six people several hours to put it back up, he adds. Then, in a suddenly serious voice, Ishen says, "It always takes less time to destroy things in life than to build them up." He says this as if to no one in particular, but I swear he is speaking to Phil and me. I swear.

The next morning I pull Phil aside and we both do a lot of apologizing. It feels good to make peace. We might not know the answer each time a shepherd asks us what we are looking for, but fighting surely isn't it. We might not be able to leave our bodies like Ishen, but—like him—we can at least act decently toward each other and the people around us.

◆ ◆ ◆

On the last full day of our trip, making our descent out of the mountains, something disturbing happens. We come upon a forested slope so steep we have to lead our horses down carefully on foot. Making matters worse, the fir trees are particularly thick, and a deep carpet of slippery needles lies underfoot. For perhaps half a mile, men and horses are slipping and sliding and glancing off branches in a confusion of meandering, crisscrossing descents. At last, we stumble out of the forest and into a meadow, everyone safe.

But there is a problem.

"Where's your whip?" Ishen asks me.

I can't find it. I search my saddle furiously, then the grass around my horse. Nothing. I panic. I remember having the whip at the top of the slope. Clearly, on the way down, I've lost it. Ishen tells me not to go back up the slope searching for it. Ten thousand men could comb that vast mountainside for days for something so small in such a tangle of trees and pine needles.

Desperate, I try anyway, but soon give up when I can't even discern our horses' tracks. I've *really* lost my whip.

"How much bad luck will I have?" I ask Ishen.

"It's just a superstition," he says, trying to console me.

"How much?"

"I don't know," he finally admits. "I have never lost a whip before." Nor, it turns out, has anyone he knows—no family members, no friends, no one. "We are so afraid of what will happen," he says, "we keep very careful guard of our whips."

This is horrifying news, of course. We pitch camp next to the forest and I go to sleep in a foul mood. Two years living in Africa have taught me to take superstitions seriously. I am full of self-pity the next morning, rambling on to Phil about my impending bad luck. Ishen disappears for his morning bath, meanwhile, and to check on the horses. He is gone a long time.

He returns for breakfast announcing he is giving most of our leftover food to nearby shepherds now that the trip is ending. He is also allowing our horses extra grazing time after yesterday's hard work. My whip problems are all I can think about while Ishen, as usual, is looking after others. He is making it hard for me to sulk. For a moment, I almost resent his nonstop kindness.

"Who are you?" I finally blurt out to him, on impulse.

"What?" he says, confused. He is pulling his hair into a long, thick ponytail.

"Who are you? You just seem so unusually . . . good. What do you know that helps you be this way? It's like you *know* something."

He is immediately embarrassed by the questions and wants to change the subject. I press on, asking if he's devoted to some special philosophy or religion. And what about the business of leaving his body? Does he see himself as a shaman? A healer? A seer?

"No, no, no," he says, then shrugs. "I am who I am. I respect children and old people and animals. I help anyone who's poor. These instructions are found in Islam, Christianity, and Buddhism. This is not special Kyrgyz behavior. This is normal behavior. The goal in life is to learn something each day and to be good. This is normal."

His words are so matter-of-fact, so devoid of drama, that I suddenly feel foolish. I've been transferring extra baggage to him all along, I realize, expecting him to deliver some transcendent message. It is, no doubt, little more than a schlocky Western hankering for a Castañeda-esque experience. But Ishen is just a nice guy. He is normal. Nothing supernatural. And he is tired of talking about it. Period. I drop the subject. We finish breakfast and stand to leave the tent.

And that's when Ishen hands me my whip.

It has been hidden at his side throughout breakfast. "I didn't want you to have bad luck," he says, placing the small leather handle in my palm.

Chills run up my legs. "How . . . ?"

"This morning," he says. "I was away. I thought you noticed."

"You couldn't have," I say. I think of the thick forest, the terrible half-mile slope, the obscuring needles.

"I found it near the top," he says, "under some branches. I didn't want bad things to happen to you."

Some things in life become less understandable the more you discuss them. I only know this: There's virtually no way Ishen—or anyone else—could have located that whip. But there it was. I hold it tightly and stare at Ishen with a mix of shock and awe. My feet eventually take me out of the tent and back to my horse. For the rest of the day, I grip my whip as if it were a magical thing. Everything around me seems slightly altered. My world seems bigger. I feel rearranged inside.

Fine weather guides us out of the mountains and back to Ishen's village that day, finally ending a trip I now keep filed away in a wholly separate category in my mind. On the fringe of an empire long thought of as spiritually dead, even evil, I had found simple goodness and something more I cannot explain. "What are you looking for?" the shepherds had asked us time and again. I never knew, not for sure, until Ishen finally showed me what it was.

He made it a gift. From another world.

11

saving ishen

When Eileen Malloy returned my call she sounded harried and and hurried, but I knew I had her full attention.

"How can I help you?" asked the deputy assistant secretary for European affairs. She was calling from her sixth-floor State Department office, looking out on the Lincoln Memorial in Washington, D.C.

It was late February 1998 and the bloodletting in Kosovo was just getting underway. Malloy's office was in full-on crisis mode, trying to head off another Balkans war. But in a split second Malloy's concerns went from the international to the personal.

"Ishen Obolbekov is dying," I told her.

With those four words, I transported Malloy back to the tiny nation of Kyrgyzstan in Central Asia. A few years before, Malloy had served as U.S. ambassador to this isolated ex-Soviet republic. Like me, she had come to know the thirty-five-year-old, long-haired, self-styled mystic named Ishen.

After several astonishing treks into the mountains with him, Malloy came to describe Ishen as one of the most "thoughtful and caring" Kyrgyz people she'd ever known. Upon leaving the country, the ambassador gave Ishen a dark-brown stallion, perhaps the greatest gift one can offer the traditionally nomadic Kyrgyz people.

My own friendship with Ishen had grown deeper during the rest of my two-year stay in Kyrgyzstan. After that first epic horseback trip together, we climbed into the Tian Shan several more times. He taught me how to herd sheep on horseback, how to hunt rabbits with falcons, and how to make the proper Kyrgyz gesture of prayer at the end of a meal, hands pressed together before your face as you say "amen." For me he continued to be a moral teacher, an instructor by example who traveled the mountains speaking regularly of Buddha, Muhammad, and Christ with equal admiration and living his life like a true student of all three.

Unknown to any of us at the time, though, was this: A deadly form of tuberculosis had already begun developing in Ishen's spine. Now, almost three years later, news had reached me back in the States that this soft-spoken man, in the prime of his life, with a wife and two young children, was dying from the disease. It was a rare form of TB caused by bacteria carried in unpasteurized cow and mare's milk.

How ironic, I thought, that Ishen had once led me to the top of a gorgeous mountain waterfall and gestured down to the tumult of rushing water. "Drink a handful of this water and we Kyrgyz believe you will gain ten more years of life," he had said. We both cupped our hands and drank deeply, feeling a faint touch of immortality.

But the water from that magic waterfall had failed Ishen. He now lay in a damp and poorly heated ex-Soviet TB ward, a six-inch-long wound on his back oozing yellow fluid from a badly botched first surgery. A second, against-all-odds surgery was now scheduled.

Ambassador Malloy and I had both recently returned to the D.C. area, and now the sudden news of Ishen's tragic decline was about to throw our lives into a desperate scramble to do something—anything—to help save our far-away friend.

And do it fast.

Rare is the veteran of overseas work who hasn't faced a situation similar to this. No matter the profession—journalism, diplomacy, missionary work, business—we inevitably make deep, personal connections with at least a small number of local people abroad . . . individuals who approach the status of family. And the ties that bind don't dissolve once we return home and put away the scrapbooks. Indeed, at the end of our careers, when all is said and done, perhaps the one true contribution we expats make to international relations comes, simply enough, when an old friend abroad needs our help.

Before calling Malloy that morning I had received an E-mail from a Canadian acquaintance in Kyrgyzstan saying Ishen had shrunk to near skeletal weight. The pain in his back had begun the year before, in the spring, and by summer he couldn't ride a horse. By fall, he was languishing in the hospital, the slightest movement sending his voice echoing in screams down chilly hallways, his wife and children helplessly standing by.

Having suffered one failed operation for his tuberculosis, he was now scheduled for a second, horrifying surgery. Poorly equipped surgeons were going to operate on his spine from the front, unzipping his abdomen and parting his organs in one of the bloodiest procedures imaginable. I was familiar with the operation because my uncle had died from similar surgery on his arthritic spine. My uncle's surgery had been performed at a first-rate U.S. hospital. How could Ishen possibly survive where he was?

The surgery was scheduled for a few days hence. "Do *not* let them operate!" I E-mailed back to my friend in Kyrgyzstan. "Tell the surgeons to wait. Tell them anything. Just give me forty-eight hours to figure something out."

That's when I called Ambassador Malloy.

"We've got to get Ishen to an American hospital," I told her.

"You're right," she said. "But that's not going to be easy."

After a pause, she said, "I can personally cover his airfare here."

"I'll make calls to doctors in the D.C. area," I offered.

But the money for medical treatment, which might soar to hundreds of thousands of dollars, would have to come from someone much, much wealthier than either of us. We had only one lead and it was a long shot. Ann Wright, of Bentonville, Arkansas, had served as the administrative officer at the U.S. embassy in Kyrgyzstan and had trekked with Ishen in the mountains and grown to admire him deeply. Wright, coincidentally, was close friends with Christy Walton, the independently wealthy daughter-in-law of Sam Walton of the Wal-Mart fortune.

Reaching Walton through Wright was critical. But there was a problem: Wright was incommunicado, serving as charge d'affaires for the U.S. embassy in Sierra Leone in the midst of a hot and ugly civil war where rebels were cutting off the heads and limbs of their enemies.

Telephone contact with Wright was nearly impossible. I had tried unsuccessfully through the State Department all morning.

Ambassador Malloy had an old E-mail address for Wright and said she'd try to reach her that way. Then Malloy said she had to go. Her boss was waiting for her at another Kosovo meeting. We'd work on our parts of the Ishen puzzle and get back to each other.

The clock was ticking.

I hung up the phone and again thought of Ishen. I remembered how much he had influenced my life. As a writer I'm trained to be skeptical of any phenomenon I can't experience firsthand through the use of my own senses. So I didn't believe in miracles until that morning in the mountains when Ishen handed me my hopelessly lost riding whip and I felt the leather handle against my own palm, still warm from Ishen's touch.

And then there was the business of his ability to predict, from time to time, my casually unannounced visits to his home. He'd already have the food set out and the tea water hot and ready to pour. But the best part was simply Ishen himself, with his handsome Eastern looks and quiet generosity. We shared that greatest mystery of all—the miracle of love—that is at the core of all deep friendships.

But now it would take yet another miracle to save Ishen's life. My wife, Catherine, who'd worked with the Peace Corps in Kyrgyzstan, made contact with a neurosurgeon at Georgetown University in D.C. The surgeon said he needed all of Ishen's medical records translated from Russian and faxed to him, an undertaking that Catherine dove into with E-mails and faxes to Kyrgyzstan.

Meanwhile, I'd still been unable to reach Ann Wright in West Africa. At one point, a State Department official in Washington, who finally reached her on a special phone line, called me, saying, "I have Ann Wright on the other line. I'm patching you through." But the connection abruptly failed and we never came as close again.

It was becoming clear that I would have to contact Walton myself, a woman I'd never met. Although Walton had met Ishen briefly in Kyrgyzstan and had even hosted him and several other Kyrgyz artisans during a special cultural visit to California, I dreaded calling her with such an enormous request.

But time was running out. With Ambassador Malloy's help I tracked down Walton's unlisted number on the West Coast. Meanwhile, other pieces of the puzzle were falling into place. A Canadian gold-mining company operating in Kyrgyzstan had agreed to fly Ishen for free on its weekly charter flight to London. Ambassador Malloy would book a ticket the rest of the way, getting a business class seat so Ishen could recline his damaged back. A registered nurse coming to the United States on home leave from duty in Kyrgyzstan volunteered to fly by Ishen's side the whole way, cleaning his terrible back wound along the way.

But everything depended on Christy Walton. I took a deep breath, preparing to tell her she was the last critical link in saving Ishen's life. Without her, Ishen would surely die. What a terrible responsibility to place—point-blank—on a person I didn't even know. But I had little choice.

Walton was suddenly on the telephone line. "Hello, Ms. Walton?" I said, feeling my heart race. "We've never met, but Ishen Obolbekov, back in Kyrgyzstan . . . he's . . . he's . . . dying."

I explained the situation. When I finished, Walton said she appreciated my call and then asked for a moment to deliberate with her husband.

"Mike?" she said, returning. "Yes, we'll take care of Ishen. If you can get him to the United States, we'll do the rest."

I hung up the phone, and my wife and I danced in and out of every room of our house.

Ishen survived the ten-thousand-mile trip to America. I'm not sure how, but he did. He was lucid but in pain when the ambulance Christy Walton had arranged picked him up upon his arrival. Owing to one of many twists of great fortune, the surgery was performed at a noted West Coast university medical center. A few years before, Walton's young son had been treated for a rare cancer at the center, eventually leading to the school's receipt of a generous grant from the Waltons and leaving the family well connected to the university staff. Ten minutes after my call to Walton, the head of the school's neurosurgery staff was calling my wife on his cell phone from freeway traffic.

Ishen's operation was a success. After a few days of tests and careful strategizing, surgeons excised the tubercular growth from his spine by deftly entering from his back, not through his abdomen. They were forced to remove some bone material from the spine during the six-hour procedure, but without impairing neurological function.

I called Ishen several hours after the procedure. He was groggy and in pain but, characteristically, it wasn't long before he changed the subject away from himself.

"Did you know," he said in a labored whisper, "that people here drink tea with ice in it? 'Ice tea,' they call it. This is crazy, ice tea."

I laughed.

Saving Ishen

"Thank you," Ishen then said abruptly. "Thank you for everything that you have done for me."

"It's nothing," I said, refusing to take any great credit for what happened.

But during our next phone conversation Ishen again went on with the thank-yous and I had to stop him by telling a story. Twelve years earlier, I explained, I almost died serving as a Peace Corps volunteer in the Congo. I had schistosomiasis and didn't know it—didn't know the parasites of this deadly disease were ravaging my liver, my intestines, my kidneys, until it was almost too late. When the 104-degree temperature struck accompanied by diarrhea drenched in blood, there were no phones to call for a rescue from my isolated village. My friend Mbaya Bukasa and a handful of other village neighbors saved my life, pouring cold water on me, keeping me awake, giving me herbal tea. I would not have made it without them or the Belgian mission nuns who eventually gave me medical treatment. It is a debt I cannot repay, although, with Ishen, I passed on part of the gift that had been given to me.

Ishen's rescue, likewise, was a true group effort involving Walton and a still-expanding group of Americans in the Washington area. Catherine, my wife, worked especially hard sorting out various medical details and writing a daily E-mail "newsletter" updating Ishen's condition for concerned individuals in Washington and around the world. There was also my friend Kitty in D.C., a former Peace Corps volunteer in Mali. When I first told her of Ishen's illness, she promptly sat down, wrote out a check, and handed it to me. This for a man she'd never met. That check paid for the many, many phone calls I made to Ishen—sometimes three a day—during his three-week stay at the West Coast hospital.

Other help poured in. We finally reached Wright in Africa, who sent money to help Ishen's family during his long absence. An international aid consultant, Rick Gaynor, who'd met Ishen in Kyrgyzstan, did the same. My friend Jack, a veteran of overseas relief work who knew Ishen only through my stories, stood before his Maryland church congregation and asked members to pray for Ishen during Sunday service. This act, more than anything else, seemed to lift Ishen's post-operative spirits.

"It's odd," Ambassador Malloy told me after the surgery, "but many of us go abroad with the goal of projecting U.S. culture. But we wind up adopting the foreign culture's values instead. Kyrgyz culture is based on a deep respect for the group, pulling together for the group. And when we all come back to America, I think we still feel responsible for the group. We're changed. That's why we all helped Ishen, I think, in every way we could."

In the end, the only reward everyone sought was granted: Ishen recovered fully. My Canadian friend in Kyrgyzstan, who'd watched the whole rescue effort unfold, later wrote me, "I never really understood what people meant about 'The American Dream.' But now I know."

Ishen spent the last week of his convalescence at my Maryland home. It was Easter week, and the symbolism wasn't lost on anyone. We drank endless bowls of hot Kyrgyz tea and Ishen made gifts of sketches he drew depicting his long odyssey—an eye overflowing with tears, a sick man lying in darkness, and finally a horse running free through a mountain meadow.

Playfully, he scolded me for my busy American lifestyle. "You do too much here. You hop around from activity to activity like this thing for your TV—what is it? Remote control?"

As Ishen became stronger and the doctors urged him to walk more, we went on excursions to the Capitol rotunda, museums, and the National Zoo. Ishen was particularly taken by the zoo's birds of prey similar to those his father still trains and uses to hunt game in the mountains of Kyrgyzstan.

The day before he flew home, Easter Sunday, we had a party. Ambassador Malloy came over, we put out a spread of food in the backyard, and my friend Jack pulled out his bagpipes and played "Amazing Grace" in the warm April sunshine. Ishen stood on my back porch and his eyes dampened. "Before, I was sick and dying in my country," he told me. "I had nothing. And now I have everything. Why is life like this? Why did everyone help me?"

"People love you very much," I said. "That's why this happened. Besides, for me, I owed you a favor for finding my riding whip back in the mountains. You saved me from a lot of bad luck, and maybe you gave me just enough good luck to help bring you here to get well. It all worked out."

He smiled and his long hair brushed against my shoulders as he gave me a hug.

IV
North of the Border, south of the Border

12
Marooned on a Desert Island

The mail boat should have been here hours ago. From my stool in Blind Sonny Lloyd's tiny waterfront bar, I can see past a stand of co-conut palms to the wooden deck where the boat was to have picked me up. Against a sunset sky, a quartet of pelicans sails over the dock and out to sea, beating wings above gin-clear water ornamented with coral reefs and the splash of bottlenose dolphins. Blind Sonny plays gospel songs on a squeeze box while I drink Bahamian beer.

"It's definitely not coming today," he says of the mail boat, pausing between songs. "Maybe it'll come tomorrow."

I'm waiting on Barreterre Cay, on the southern end of the Bahamas's Ex-uma Cays. Barreterre is a stop on the Bahamian mail boat circuit, and in the-ory a ship stops here weekly carrying cargo, mail, and passengers between

Nassau and the other islands. Mail boats are the conveyance of choice for poor Bahamians and the occasional backpacker. My goal, if the boat ever comes, is to hop on board, sail 110 miles southeast along a forgotten archipelago of sun-kissed cays, and get myself marooned on a desert island. That's "marooned," as in stranded, and "desert," as in sand dunes, cactuses, wind-blown palms, spectacular lagoons and beaches, maybe an iguana or two.

This attractive and probably ill-advised mission is partly mundane: a chance to dodge the ice and cold of a D.C. winter. It's also a test. Travel writer laureate Paul Theroux is fond of claiming that even in a shrinking world of mass tourism, genuinely obscure landscapes and cultures still exist for the determined traveler. Examining a map of the West Indies in my living room one freezing December night, I decided to take Theroux at his word. My eyes tripped over a microscopic raft of land called Ragged Island, 250 miles southeast of Nassau, all alone on the far edge of the Great Bahama Bank. The two-by-five-mile island bore a single settlement: Duncan Town, population eighty-nine.

Getting any additional information about Ragged Island soon proved nearly impossible. I consulted the guidebook *Hidden Bahamas,* which specializes in part in getting travelers off the beaten track—but not a single mention of Ragged Island. I called the Bahamas Out-Islands Promotion Board in Fort Lauderdale, Florida. "Never heard of it," said a woman named Maura. "We have zero information on the place. Sorry."

But this much I learned quickly: There are no commercial flights to Ragged Island. Unless you have your own yacht, which I emphatically do not, or you can charter a plane, which I can't afford, then the only way to get on and off this unfrequented, end-of-the-line place sixty-five miles from Cuba is by mail boat. And the more I learned about the extremely erratic ways of Bahamian mail boats, the more I realized that having one drop you off on an island with the promise of picking you up a week later is very much a way of getting stuck. Which is to say marooned.

Even here on Barreterre, a lovely cay on the more trammeled Bahamian path and a key stop on the Nassau-to-Duncan Town mail run, no one knows anything about Ragged Island. "Sorry, mon," says Blind Sonny. "I never been there. Don't think I know anyone who has. Probably just fishermen there." A shopkeeper next door did see the island, as a kid, from the distant remove of a sponge-diving boat. But that, he tells me, was almost seventy years ago.

I might not get there either, of course, if the mail boat doesn't come pick me up. It might come tomorrow. It might come in a week. The boats are famous for breaking down.

According to my pre-trip research, one person who *had* been to Ragged Island was none other than Christopher Columbus—on his maiden voyage to the new world. How paradoxical that one of the first places visited by European explorers still lies completely off the obscurity charts five hundred years later. In a way, too, Columbus sailed the very first mail boat of the West Indies, hopping from island to island, picking up supplies, dropping off men. In early 1493, Columbus left most of his crew on the island of Hispaniola and raced back to Spain to report his find. When he returned in late 1493, fully stocked with new supplies and, presumably, at least a few letters for the men, he could not find any of the thirty-nine stranded crew members. They had all died of disease. Or they'd been murdered.

"Hey, mon, I think you missed your boat!" the bartender yells to me.

Different day, different bar, same thing: I've been waiting all morning with my gear—and still no boat.

"She just passed by," the bartender says, pointing out to sea. "The tide's too low here right now. She's decided to go straight to Ragged Island!"

I blink, uncomprehending: You mean even when the boat comes, it doesn't stop?

Two sympathetic carpenters drinking rum see me banging my head against a table with alarming force. They heroically grab my gear and lead me to a seventeen-foot Boston whaler. To my amazement, we're soon heading out to sea across pounding waves, spray dampening our clothes, closing in on the eighty-foot mail boat that has the vague look of a big, beat-up shrimp boat.

It's steaming toward open water and a sinking sun when someone throws down a ladder and I climb up.

On board at last.

The carpenters refuse money, waving good-bye as a crew member with dreadlocks leads me to a small cabin with six bunks. The cabin's all mine, he says. There are only three passengers on the boat. Only three human beings in the whole world traveling to Ragged Island this week—me and two Bahamians. The crew outnumber us by more than two to one.

I stash my gear, noticing out my port window the island of Great Exuma fading to a dot in a sea of stunning emerald. I go on deck to inspect the boat, amazed at what I find: From stem to stern the entire rig's made of wood. No steel-and-rivets gunwales. No fiberglass hull. Just wood planking.

"She's one of the last wooden boats in the whole Bahamian mail boat fleet," says first mate Cephas Maycock. He's in the wheelhouse, barefoot, steering us at a groaning ten mph toward far-off Ragged Island. "By law, all the new mail boats, they have to be made of steel."

There's a definite chewing-gum-and-baling-wire feel to the vessel. Cephas, thirty-eight, says he's more than a day behind schedule because an engine alternator went out in Nassau and he couldn't fix it or replace it. If the engines cut off, he'll have a heck of a time restarting them at sea.

As for not stopping at Barreterre, Cephas apologizes—but I'm not mad. I'm on board now, ticket in pocket, a warm trade wind riffling through my clothes. From the wheelhouse deck, I look straight down through fourteen feet of water to an ocean floor of delicately rippled sand. Two giant stingrays wing past with utter grace; a translucent jellyfish pulses toward the calm surface. The green, luminous water goes on forever, stretching till the Earth's curvature stops the eye just below a tangerine sun.

Through the open wheelhouse door, Cephas finally begins to unwrap the mystery of Ragged Island.

"I'm *from* Ragged Island," he tells me. "Born and raised there. The island used to be four hundred people, thanks to the salt flats and a sisal plantation.

But that's all died away now and we're less than one hundred people—fisher-men and lobster divers is all. I've steered mail boats all over the Bahamas and this island is the most far away. The people are the loneliest."

And any visitors? I ask. Cephas laughs: the odd backpacker and the very, very occasional yacht. The island's not on the way to anywhere. No one comes.

And beaches? "Very nice beaches on Ragged Island," he says. "Very, very nice beaches."

These words are still on my mind as, by moonlight, I head down the deck ladder to my room, open my cabin window to the breeze, and let the boat rock me to sleep.

I awake at six-thirty to stillness. We've arrived—and already cargo is moving off the boat. A flotilla of fishermen in eighteen-foot outboards has motored out to meet the mail boat, which is anchored offshore. Behind the fishing boats is Ragged Island itself, all scrub trees and limestone bluffs with Duncan Town spread across one hillside. The town's a ramble of wobbly docks and thirty mostly old and sun-bleached buildings, no two the exact same shade of pastel: pink, green, blue, yellow.

Eagerly, I lower my gear and myself into one of the fishing boats, which have come laden with bounty: fifty-pound bags of lobster, conch, and grouper for shipment to distant markets. They return with staples from planet Nassau. My boat carries bunches of green plantains, sacks of potatoes, PVC pipe, a stereo.

With some apprehension, I wave good-bye to the mail boat crew. By noon they'll weigh anchor, blow a horn, and head back to Nassau, returning—maybe—in a week. "But don't worry, mon," says the fisherman now taking me through a mangrove swamp toward Duncan Town. "Even when the mail boat breaks down, I've never known her to be more than three weeks late."

I finger the wad of U.S. twenties in my pocket, figuring I'll be scrubbing boat hulls for my supper by then.

Amid the hive of greeters and straw-hatted revelers on the Duncan Town quay (it's a day-long party whenever the mail boat calls here) is Angela

Munroe, the island postmistress. She's dressed in shorts and flip-flops. The mail bag's already come ashore, and I'm curious: "How many letters came here this week?"

She eyes me a bit sheepishly. "Five," she says, then adds that three are for the island's Guyanese schoolteacher. "Many weeks we get no mail," she says. "The boat brings us nothing."

I'm officially marooned now, walking past scattered coconut palms and palmettos and up a steep hill into town. No thatch-roofed cabanas with rainbow-colored drinks here. I have but one lodging choice: a small, clean room over a fishermen's bar called the Ponderosa. The bar's already throbbing with calypso music at 8:00 A.M. But what a view! A deep wicker chair on my second-floor veranda faces miles of unbroken ocean.

I unpack to the sound of rolling combers mixed with roosters crowing and the thump of my closest neighbor pounding fresh conch flesh to hang and dry on a clothesline. So what if my shower runs cold and brackish and is activated by a crescent wrench? I'm stuck here and feeling happier by the moment.

It is a centuries-old custom of shipwrecked sailors to survey their domain as a first step, thus confirming the dawning suspicion: It's an island you're on and there's no way off. And like Robinson Crusoe, I can survey my island from a single hilltop. The hill's just outside town, along the single transisland road. Like the rest of this limestone dot of land, it's covered with the scrubby, prickly vegetation common to the southern Bahamas: thorn trees, scattered cactuses, aloe vera, tangled bushes, and curling vines. The ubiquitous thorns speak of a scant existence, of scorching sun and ocean wind and parched soil. Yes, indeed: It's a desert island.

The hill reveals an eponymously ragged coastline with stunning pale-green water and reefs on three sides. To the far north, a series of tiny uninhabited cays (the Ragged Island Range) stretch back to the main Bahamas archipelago more than one hundred miles away. To the west is a jumble of meandering cliffs and deep limestone caves. And in several directions my eyes find the beaches. Within five minutes I'm on a lonesome smile of sand, unlacing my shoes. Soon I'm a cliche in sunglasses and rolled-up pant legs, my feet on talcum sand that has the slightest hint of pink, fringed by untrammeled sea grass and dunes.

I walk and walk and walk. I see nurse sharks mating in the shallows, and I walk some more. I watch a gigantic hawksbill turtle surface in a lagoon. I read and swim and walk some more. I fall asleep and wake up hungry.

There's only one restaurant on Ragged Island, Sheila's Fisherman's Lounge, and it's always closed. I go to Sheila's whitewashed house with the mountain of lobster traps out front and ask her to open the restaurant. Wearing a blue beret above cataract-clouded eyes, old Sheila says, Why bother? There are never any customers on Ragged Island anyway. If I want food, I should just come straight to her house—which I do, day after day, slipping through her kitchen door to buy plates of fried lobster and turtle stew and big slabs of grouper.

After evening meals, I wander the narrow streets of Duncan Town in the golden honey of the Bahamian sunset. People are on their front porches, gripping fly swatters and swaying atop crude hammocks made from discarded fish netting. The islanders grin and wave at me and my outsider exotica: Look at that fanny pack!

Anyone can beach a yacht on one of a thousand uninhabited West Indian islands and say, "Here I am! All alone!" But if all you want is to be by yourself on a microdot of land, a weekday picnic at a place like D.C.'s Roosevelt Island would surely save you some trouble. A better challenge is to engage people—to find a culture that is itself an island off the beaten path. And that's certainly what I find on Ragged Island. Paul Theroux is no liar.

The island men are old-school fishermen, tossing out spools of handheld line from small boats to hook thirty-pound grouper and fang-toothed barracuda. Or they hold their breath and dive fifteen feet to skewer reef lobsters with a simple, lethal spear called a Hawaiian sling. The women raise kids and dry laundry on rope clotheslines and weave palm-frond baskets in a style first used by slaves 250 years ago. Numerous people still administer "bush medicine," brewing teas from island bushes and always using an odd number of bushes, never even, or it won't work.

Midweek, I get a sore throat and seventy-year-old Garnella Armrister helps me make one of these soothing teas. "I cured myself of TB drinking this," she says. She lives with her blind husband, Steven, in a tilting, two-story stucco home with a wood-shingle roof. Like most of the island homes, gravity-flow plumbing brings rainwater inside from an outdoor cistern. Garnella's grandchildren go to the pink one-room schoolhouse on the village's far edge. It's past the police station fringed with red-blooming oleander flowers, where two extremely bored officers oversee a perpetually empty steel-bar cell. Nearby is the home of the island's sole Cuban refugee, a man who left a Nassau detention center and took the mail boat to the most hidden place he could find. He began fishing here like everyone else, selling his fare on the mail boat from the safe obscurity of an island where no one cares where you're from.

There are no computers on Ragged Island. Nor are there cell phones. Nor has a cruise ship ever called here. Three bars and three churches proffer vice and virtue in equal measure. At night I drop my beer money into Cuban cigar boxes atop sticky wood-plank counters. On Sunday, I drop a cash offering in a wicker basket to the peculiar Bahamian crash of gospel tambourines and cymbals in a one-room sanctuary with weathered shutters open to the ocean breeze.

But even here, on Ragged Island, the world is drawing closer. Electricity came in 1995, and already many islanders are joining that strange stratum of the Third World: satellite TV owners with outhouses. And absurdly, there are four rusting pickup trucks, a motorcycle and three golf-cart-like vehicles—all brought in by barge—that trundle Duncan Town's less than one mile of roads.

Still, the profound feeling of apartness is little disturbed. During my evening walks, that feeling gradually yields to full-blown loneliness and a sense of sadness settling over this desert island. The stiff trade wind hums and howls mournfully through Duncan Town as I stroll, whistling past the abandoned houses of all those who've decamped for the outside world. The wind blows perpetually on Ragged Island—blows and blows and blows, coming uninterrupted through the Mira Por Vos Passage, creating what some here call the "wind capital of the world" and littering eastern beaches with the flotsam of far-flung trash. The plaintive howl fills my ears as sea water darkens all around, stretching away infinitely and in every direction, leaving me appalled all over again at how cleanly isolated from the greater universe this land raft is, with no way off till the mail boat comes again. If it ever comes again.

Up ahead, scratchy calypso and reggae music spill from the Hilltop View Bar, my favorite. I buy a beer and stretch out on a fish-net hammock under some palms across the street. The wind rattles through the fronds as a fragrant hint of marijuana floats up from a nearby dock.

"Our country has forgotten this island," says Rafael, the bartender, lying in a hammock next to me because business is slow. "The government won't dredge the channel. They say we're too small and far away. We should just abandon the island and come to Nassau, they say. It's like we're lost at sea, mon. Forgotten. Lost."

The wind carries his words away and I fall asleep, waking up hours later to find the whole village has gone to bed without me. All lights are out. Groggily, I shuffle to my rough ocean-view room, a weave of hammock lines crisscrossing one side of my face.

No one will rent me a bicycle on Ragged Island. "Just take it and bring it back when you're done," people say. So I hop on an orange relic with foot brakes and fat tires and head for the south side of the island to meet an eccentric outsider named Percy Wilson. Nine years ago, a drug-smuggling plane overran the island airstrip (no airport, just an unlit runway for emergencies) and crashed. Percy somehow dragged the DC-3 out of the mangrove swamp, pushed it to the beach, and turned it into a home for his family and a bar for fishermen passing by this side of the island. He gives me a tour of the "upstairs"—cocktail tables running the length of the fuselage—and the walled-in "downstairs" where an old jukebox sits below the landing-gear cavity.

Like everyone on the island, Percy is a fisherman, and after morning juice under the DC-3 nose cone, he takes me out for his daily catch. Soon, we're both taking deep breaths and diving in ten feet of water, Hawaiian slings in hand, spearing lobster and grouper amid a panorama of coral. I swim past staghorn forests, delicate branching corals, purple sea fans, and golden brain corals the size of boulders. This whole south side of the island, a good two miles from Duncan Town, has a magical wilderness feel, completely uninhabited except for Percy and his family in the DC-3.

Later we eat lobster under the nose cone, and Percy, who wears a braided goatee, introduces me to his pet raccoon, Cherokee, and tells me he brews a bush tea called "Naked Man" to bolster the immune system. I ask him if he ever gets lonely.

"Lonely for what?" he says. "Everything we need is right here. Food from the sea. Clean air. When I go to Nassau, that's when I get sick and lonely."

It's something I hear from everyone on Ragged Island. Those people temperamentally unsuited for the solitary fisherman's life have already departed, leaving behind a group of islanders who, forgotten or not by the rest of the world, are admirably satisfied with their lot, with the routines of their lives.

"Going out to sea is an adventure I can never get enough of," says fisherman Alvin Munroe the next day, motioning toward his Malabu whaler with its assortment of spears, a rusting trident, giant fish hooks, and a spool of thirty-pound test line.

To prove his point, Alvin promptly guides me out to my own excellent adventure, carefully poling his boat toward a school of ten thousand bonefish along a sand-bottom flat north of the island. Before me is a sportsman's dream: bonefish everywhere, bonefish beyond comprehension. We eat a quick breakfast of raw conch plucked straight from the water and doused with hot pepper and lemon juice. Then we wade into the water and start reeling in bonefish, one after another, some exceeding five pounds. Alvin uses his spool while I fish with the only sport rod on the island, tossing out strange flies cut from frayed denim jeans. But these work, the boat fills with fish, and we finally quit when our arms get too tired to go on.

Topping off this great day, Alvin passes on some surprising news: He heard on Radio Bahamas that the Ragged Island mail boat was leaving Nassau on time. In two days, in principle, it will reach Ragged Island. I knock twice on the wooden shaft of Alvin's trident spear and start cleaning bonefish.

At 6:00 A.M. Thursday I leap to my veranda and look north and sure enough: There's the mail boat anchored in the bay. A miracle. I'm happy, and not happy: I've got to leave now. Any thoughts of staying another week are dashed by fears that a week could easily become a month. It was hard enough just getting here. Why tempt fate and my limited cash reserves?

On board, first mate Cephas is proud to be on schedule for the first time in three weeks. I got lucky. The weather was good coming down, and he got a new alternator from Miami so he can turn off his engines without fear of being stranded at sea in this old wooden boat.

Pulling away, I feel increasingly regretful. Despite some drawbacks (the wind blows a bit too hard for my tastes) and hardships, this island flirts with paradise status, physically and culturally. Of all the places I've visited on the globe, I've never felt safer than on Ragged Island, where locks rust from disuse, people provide help without thinking of money and a whole island can go to bed without the slightest concern for the foolhardy foreigner conked out in a streetside hammock.

As it turns out, I'm the only passenger on the mail boat this time. I stash my gear in a tiny cabin and later recall something Percy had told me after our lobster dive as we waded ashore under the lavish Bahamian sun. "Think about what kind of world we'd have if every kid on the planet could grow up on an island like this. There'd be no more violence, mon. No more hatred. Just love for everybody. A big, big love."

147

If only Ragged Island could gobble up the rest of the world instead of sliding slowly in the opposite direction, maybe we could all be stranded together. Marooned as a way of life, with the world as one big island.

And maybe, we wouldn't need mail boats anymore.

13
Montreal, Expos'd

Hundreds of crazed fans in this crowd of five thousand foreigners begin standing and savagely slamming the backs of their chairs up and down, up and down to register their intense approval of what's happening on the playing field. The act creates sharp explosions of sound not unlike small-arms fire. The only people not banging chairs, it seems, are the sticky-fingered children eating deep-fried pancakes called Beaver Tails or forking up strange mounds of French fries laced with cheese and slathered with gravy.

Suddenly, down on the field halfway through this *"match,"* something bad happens for the home team. The French-speaking fans begin yelling at the mostly Spanish-speaking players: *"Pourri! Pourri!* Rotten! Rotten!" People whistle and blow on long, booming plastic horns that remind me of a European soccer contest even though the sport on display was invented 150 years ago in the United States.

North of the Border, South of the Border

I am, of course, taking in a Major League Baseball game in Montreal, Canada. I'm watching the pinstriped Expos on their home turf, a nine-inning experience that's perhaps the best multicultural adventure available to North American fans of an "Anglo" nature. It's a spectacle up here, a combination of God's two greatest inventions: baseball and foreign travel. As a junkie of both, I'm borderline apoplectic, immersed in fastballs and home runs, foreign billboards and surnames I can't pronounce.

But a worrisome question nags as I sip my Molson: Do we Americans really want these guys? Unless you're totally tone-deaf to sports news, you probably know the perennial speculation that the financially troubled Expos may eventually move south of the border to Charlotte, North Carolina, or Washington, D.C., or even Fairfax, Virginia.

So I've come here as more than a sports tourist. I'm on a scouting mission, crossing the border for a sneak preview. I've already told my two-year-old son, an emerging fan back home, that this is his team. He wears a tiny Expos hat when we play Whiffle ball in the backyard.

But seeing this team firsthand reveals the naked truth: They're *awful.* Just now, an Expos batter strikes out on four pitches against the Philadelphia Phillies, triggering grumbles from the sparse crowd at Olympic Stadium. The team mascot—an orange and hairy something called Youppi (French for "hooray")—leads the fans in more chair-slamming fun, trying to keep a rally alive.

The next batter runs the count full, teasing the fans, before popping out to the pitcher. More grumbles. The Expos in 1999 have the lowest team payroll in baseball and some of the youngest players—and they are off to one of their worst starts in the team's thirty-year history. Two nights ago, the players committed six errors in a single game.

Expos second baseman Wilton Guerrero steps to the plate as Youppi waves his hirsute arms wildly and the fans begin yelling things in French I can't understand. Guerrero, like the rest of the team, is in a terrible slump, and he falls behind in the count just as I come to a realization: Whatever happens in this game, I'll leave without regrets. If the Expos decamp for the United States, this will be one of the last summers to see French Canadian big league base-ball, a phenomenon worth catching before it goes, if for no other reason than it provides something found nowhere else in North America: minor league baseball with major league players.

For anyone fashionably tired of big pro salaries, high ticket prices, arrogant players, and the hassle of big crowds, the Expos offer the best of all worlds. I took a cheap Air Canada flight here, spent two days wandering around one of the world's great cities, and now I'm getting the farm league treatment: a tiny crowd, players barely old enough to shave, a crazy marriage proposal in the stands brokered by the mascot, and a wooden outfield scoreboard with num-bers updated manually by teenagers. All this for the ridiculously low ticket price of less than $5 U.S. and a seat so close to the action that I can almost smell the pine tar.

Guerrero bounces to second for an out, ending the inning. I do the only sensible thing. I order another Molson.

My innkeeper in downtown Montreal, Madeline, says in accented English, "So what if the Expos leave town? There are many things *fantastique* and unique in Montreal besides just the Expos."

She's right, of course, and I'm determined see some of those fantastic things before hitting the ballpark.

I begin by renting a mountain bike and pedaling straight to the top of Mont Royal, the dramatic, forested mountain (okay, a big hill) in the dead center of town that gives the city its name. A winding gravel road takes me through stands of Canadian maples to a beautiful summit park designed by Frederick Law Olmsted. It's odd to stand at the grassy pinnacle and be eyeball to eyeball with the tops of skyscrapers just ten blocks away.

On the way down, pausing for great views of the lovely St. Lawrence River, I pass a pair of oddly segregated cemeteries—one for French speakers, one for English speakers—a site that mutely summarizes the long-festering cultural divisions within Quebec.

The next day is game day. I visit the Old Fort on St. Helen's Island in the middle of the St. Lawrence River before heading to Olympic Stadium. After the War of 1812, the British prepared for a possible American invasion of Montreal by building this moated fortress with eight-foot-long cannons and two-meter-thick stone walls. As something of an invader myself, I grow slightly self-conscious inside those walls. Maybe I'm paranoid, but the eyes of those period-dress sentries make me think they're onto me, pegging me as the expeditionary fingertip of America's long arm reaching up to snatch the Expos. I make a discreet but hasty exit.

Back on terra firma, there's time for one more stop. I arrive two hours early at Le Stade Olympique, leaving plenty of time to hit Moe's Deli and Bar, where Expos fans gather. It's a friendly place with exposed-brick walls, barbecued ribs, and desserts kept in an old phone booth by the bar. It's happy hour—two-for-one Labatt beers right up till game time, perhaps to anesthetize the fans for the poor play sure to follow.

I sit at the bar next to Daniel, a baseball-hatted Expos loyalist, who has a message for American fans. "Don't accept our Expos," he tells me.

I let him know I'm from the D.C. area and he grows even more emphatic.

"You've lost two teams of your own [the Senators], so you know what it feels like. Please don't do this to us."

I grimace and finish my second Labatt and push back my stool while Daniel, like all Montrealers I meet, remains a friendly sport to the end.

"When you reach the stadium," he says, "buy the cheapest ticket in the house. It's only seven dollars Canadian [$4.80 U.S.]. Then, after the first pitch, sit wherever you want."

"A seven-dollar seat, please," I tell the stadium ticket seller moments later, handing over my money. I walk through the turnstile, past the popcorn and pennant venders, toward Section 139, right field. Virtually alone in my area, I take in batting practice amid thoroughly modern trappings: artificial turf, a space-age stadium roof, a gargantuan replay screen in center field. But already it doesn't quite feel like major league baseball.

First, of course, there's the ticket price, about a quarter of what you'd pay at most Major League parks. Then there's the action on the field. An Expos coach is pitching batting practice using a wobbly shopping cart full of baseballs, and he's throwing to the beat of French rock music blasting over the P.A. Thirty feet below me, two teenage boys are standing on a crude scaffold, diligently updating a sprawling pre–World War II–type wooden scoreboard that gives results from around the league. This old-fashioned work, utterly exposed to those of us in the cheap seats, involves taking scores from a press-box official, then reaching into several wooden troughs for wooden slabs hand-painted with numbers and sliding them into the appropriate slot. One of them wears a felt Gatsby hat.

I exit the stands for a quick pregame bite. "One order of *poutine*," I tell the uniformed attendant at a concession stand. Poutine, a uniquely Quebecois concoction combining French fries, cheddar cheese, and beef-stock gravy, is so popular that it's served at McDonald's restaurants throughout the province. I watch the cook in back combine the fries and cheese in a tall paper cup, then slop on a ladleful of thick gravy from a stainless-steel vat. He pauses and then, momentarily indecisive, adds a second, heaping ladleful.

I'm back at my seat in time for the national anthem, spearing dripping mouthfuls of poutine with a fork. For extreme junk food, it's not so bad, though halfway through the serving my stomach begins making odd noises that compete with the junior high school band playing "O Canada" with tubas and French horns on the field.

The Expos take the field next, and the crowd, sprinkled more or less evenly across the stadium, begins banging empty seats up and down in preparation for the opening pitch. Twenty-five-year-old Expos pitcher Mike Thurman is on the mound, and as he warms up you can almost sense the whole place cringe. With an 0–2 record and an ERA of 8.05, he's the worst pitcher on the second-worst pitching staff in the National League. Just two nights ago, Expos pitchers gave up seventeen runs in a game.

But the first pitch from Thurman is a strike on the outside corner, and cheers go up just as the strange migration begins. True to Daniel's prediction, everyone in the stands not already seated behind home plate makes a beeline for amazingly choice (and empty) lower-level seats just twenty rows from the field (above a narrow VIP section) in an arc from dugout to dugout. I grab the rest of my poutine and join the exodus. By the end of the first inning, we fans are huddled cozily around home plate.

In the third inning, the Expos stage a mini-rally. Third baseman Mike Mordecai lines a clean single to left, and the juices start flowing in the stands. I get caught up in the excitement—this is my team, too—so I stand and begin slamming the back of my chair and cheer madly like those around me. The noise coming from these fans is, no exaggeration, as much as I've heard from crowds four times as big in other parks. Despite the high-decibel support, the rally sputters when Thurman strikes out trying to lay down a bunt.

Next to me, a serious fan named Jean Yves Leduc is studiously scoring the game. He says he's attended at least forty Expos home games every year for the past two decades. He puts down his scoring pencil and reminisces about highlights, including the twenty-two-inning game against Los Angeles in 1987 and the time he shook hands with third baseman Tim Wallach in the parking lot before a game. "I could feel all the calluses on Wallach's hand from taking extra batting practice every day," Yves says. "I'll never forget those calluses. He was so dedicated to this team and to the game."

And what will Yves do if the Expos leave town?

"I had a talk with my girlfriend," he says, "and I decided that, with all my new free time, I would just go ahead and get married and have a life."

It's the top of the fourth when Thurman makes a mistake pitch and Phillies right fielder Bobby Abreu lifts a second two-run homer into left field. Four-zip, Philadelphia.

"One more Phillies run," mutters the old farmer next to me after removing his teeth, whistling, and putting them back in, "and I'm going home to watch hockey."

Halfway through the fifth inning, Yves gets into an animated conversation with a hot dog vendor. It's all in French, and they both laugh a great deal, and

I ask Yves what's so funny. "The crowd's so small tonight that the stadium is telling all the vendors—when they go back for more hot dogs—to go home. They're getting paid for only half a game. But this vendor's decided to avoid the order by not going back to resupply. That way, he can at least get his base pay for the rest of the game."

Sure enough, the vendor walks away with a smile, barking to the crowd, "No hot dogs here! No hot dogs! *Pas de chiens chauds!*"

Unexpectedly, the Expos make a heroic comeback with three runs in the seventh, while a young relief pitcher called up from Double-A somehow keeps the Phillies scoreless. By the bottom of the ninth, the drama escalates. The Expos are down 4–3 with two outs and a man on second. First baseman Ryan McGuire, who has power, steps to the plate.

We may be few, but we fans do our best. Youppi claps his hairy orange hands and directs our cheers to the field. Chairs are banging. The vendor has stopped not selling hot dogs and is rooting like everyone else. The scoreboard guys are smoking nervously, peeping through a hole in the outfield scoreboard. The guy with the false teeth, true to his word, has stayed to the end.

On a 2–1 pitch, McGuire lifts a towering blast to left field that's clearly on its way out of the park. We jump for joy and cheer louder and louder. But the Phillies left fielder refuses to give up on the ball. He drifts back, back, back, and, incredibly, makes the catch against the outfield fence. Five thousand people collapse in their seats in anguish and disbelief.

It's over.

It was a good game, and the young Expos have no reason to drop their chins. But there is something very sad about the way these previously boisterous fans shuffle slowly out of the stadium. An unusually large number stop and linger at souvenir stands by the exit gates. *Souvenir.* A French word meaning to remember. For many of these fans, this may very well be the last time they see their Expos. They buy hats, T-shirts, pennants. To remember.

I take the Montreal subway back to downtown thinking two things. First, I sincerely hope Montreal figures out a way to keep its team and prosper, even if it means we Americans in D.C. or Charlotte or Fairfax, Virginia, don't get a squad. Second, if the Expos *do* come to Washington by some twist of fate, I can't wait for the day when I can bring my son to a game. I'll really show him how to make a stadium chair hum.

14
Peccary Hunting in the Amazon

Carrying a dead, eighty-pound, piglike animal on my back through a jungle swamp with only one shoe on my feet and thorns in my hand and mosquitoes blanketing my face and my eyeglasses fogged to uselessness—this had never been part of my plan for visiting the Amazon rain forest.

But when the outboard motor of Bolivar's dugout canoe broke for the second and final time that afternoon, our agenda changed dramatically. The original goal had been to travel fifteen miles up the Zabalo River—a distant tributary of the Amazon in the eastern jungles of Ecuador—to visit an oil well these Cofan Indians had recently burned to the ground. Twenty-six-year-old Bolivar, who wore a friendly smile on his face and a menacing bat tatoo on his upper arm, was part of a clan of seventy Cofan who were defying the illegal and highly destructive entry of oil companies onto their tribal forest land. I had come down to South America to write about the Indians' vigilante campaign and to photograph the destroyed well platform.

But it was the dry season in this part of the Amazon and the water level of the Zabalo River was extremely low, exposing all manner of fallen tree trunks and other hazards. We'd been laboriously chopping logs and portaging the canoe for most of the day when, in rapid succession, the boat motor's spark plugs grew fouled and the rip cord broke, snapping right in half.

It was too late in the day to continue on foot to the oil site, so we reluctantly scuttled the expedition. We would now have to turn around without a motor and head back to the village where we'd arrive deep in the night. Thoroughly crestfallen, my Cofan companions decided to temporarily brighten their moods by doing what they do best: hunt wild animals.

After a restorative round of banana beer along the riverbank, Bolivar's father, Elias, a soft-spoken man dressed in a traditional Indian cotton tunic, began signaling for silence. He detected some sort of noise in the forest.

"Monkeys," he said to me in Spanish, cocking his head to one side, letting his straight, black hair hang toward the ground. He was sure he heard monkeys.

He and Bolivar grabbed their single-barrel shotguns, and I followed them unarmed into the jungle. Behind me was Norma, Bolivar's beautiful wife with ruddy cheeks and midnight-black eyes. She brought our hunting party to four.

Elias led the way, shotgun on one side, machete on the other, single-handedly cutting a trail through the undergrowth as fast as he could walk, slicing and slicing, never breaking his stride. He was almost too mechanical to be real.

For a moment the sudden excitement of the quest, combined with the sun-dappled grandeur of the verdant forest, restored my flagging spirit. Fragile beams of light fell all around us, streaking through the luxuriant canopy overhead to illuminate a poetic riot of lianas and creepers and the massive trunks of kapok trees streaked with epiphytic mosses that looked like water colors—red and orange and yellow and violet.

But we soon lost the sound of the monkeys and came to a halt. The river was no longer in sight, and I wasn't sure in which direction it lay. As we stood at the end of this blind alley, wondering what went wrong, Bolivar detected the grunt of a tapir (that strange, hoofed, long-snouted animal common to the Amazon) somewhere in the distance—and suddenly we had another mammal to pursue. He and Elias put keen ears and eyes to work, probing in all directions, casting about for more clues.

Standing apart from these bronze-skinned men, watching as now they gestured and discussed in spirited Cofan which way to go, I realized that with the physical switch to the forest interior the Indians had made a shift in states of mind as well. At warp speed their senses processed hundreds of bits of data altogether hidden from me, the visiting gringo, the man doing all he could just to keep up. The Indians' presence here was as natural and as graceful as the spread of monstrous trees in every direction. These were not visitors, after all, not in a forest hosting Amerindian inhabitants for more than fifty thousand years, a stay which had nearly the aspect of geologic time. It would have been as easy to contemplate the absence of kapok trees and macaws and river dolphins here as that of Bolivar and Elias in their *ondiccuje* tunics, cupping their ears to hear their prey better, wrinkling their noses to smell the forest's clues. The men were part of the scenery. They *belonged.* It wouldn't be a proper rain forest without them.

Bolivar chose a direction and off we went in pursuit of the tapir. It was a good sign that we passed half-devoured mauritia fruit along the ground, a favorite food of both tapirs and peccaries. And now the hoofprints were so clear even I could see them. For a long time we followed the prints, pushing farther and farther into the forest, which became denser the deeper we traveled into it—and concomitantly darker. It became so dark at one point that usually nocturnal mosquitoes, thinking it their witching hour, began attacking us in swarms each time we paused.

The tapir was now taking us in and out of steep-banked muddy streams and standing pools of swampy water. Up front, Elias continued his brisk machete work, leading us to all manner of naturally fallen trees which we crawled over or under according to size. My eyeglasses kept fogging up badly, meanwhile, like a mirror after a shower—a condition brought on by my own heavy perspiration and the almost soupy forest humidity all around.

Then the tapir tracks petered out. We lost the animal. There were no more sounds to follow, either. Another dead end. Given how far we had strayed from the river, I was almost glad of this second dose of failure. Just how we would have gotten a two-hundred-pound tapir from this distant spot to the canoe was beyond me.

Yet no sooner had we made an about-face, retracing a few of our steps, then Bolivar and Elias stopped and began taking deep breaths through their noses. "Smell that?" Bolivar asked me in Spanish, still inhaling deeply. "Smell that? Peccaries. Lots of them."

I employed my nose to its fullest capacity, but failed to detect anything in the air indicating a bevy of large-tusked, wire-haired, piglike creatures was near. Not that anyone was seeking my confirmation, mind you. The next thing I knew, Bolivar, Elias, and Norma—without any notice—were disappearing in a virtual sprint to my right, fading into the jungle. Here we go again, I thought, as I commanded my legs to do everything they could to keep up.

Our quarry was very close this time, the pursuit red hot. There was no time for clearing any semblance of a trail with the machete. The rules changed to every person for himself. Leafy branches whipped across my face. Hanging vines nicked my shoulders and arms. Unseen divots in the soil caused missteps. I was aware of vague human figures bounding and darting up ahead of me, and, for fear of being abandoned more than anything, I stumbled and bumbled my way forward, staying more or less within sight of the figures.

Then, abruptly, the Cofan stopped and I reached them. Bolivar and Elias cocked their ears and whispered to each other while I tried catching my breath. But too soon, they were off again, bolting away. We splashed through a swampy area, then plunged into some very thick foliage that left an odd scratchy feeling in my throat as if, in the act of plowing face-first through the branches and leaves, I had swallowed some delicate, feathery forest thing.

We came to another steep-banked stream across which a fallen tree acted as a convenient bridge—for the Cofan. For me it was impossibly narrow. The Indians scurried across with mystifying dexterity while I threw myself into a crashing slide down one bank, sloshed through the current, then flung myself up the muddy far slope before redoubling my running pace to catch the others.

Then we stopped again. We really stopped. We stopped because we were almost on top of our prey. Bolivar and Elias stood stock-still, fingers to their lips to indicate silence as they surveyed the surroundings with their ears. This was clearly the point at which absolute stealth and quiet were at a premium, but the vexing hair ball or whatever it was lodged in my throat was threatening to jeopardize our cover. The urge to clear my windpipe with a huge, satisfying cough was almost overwhelming, and repressing it literally brought tears to my eyes. I held out as long as I could for the sake of the group, but then a short, muffled cough escaped.

Everyone turned to me with fingers pressed to their lips, eyebrows arched in anger, silently shouting at me that the peccaries were oh-so-close. I shrugged apologetically just as three very loud, full-bodied coughs burst forth which were no doubt at that moment scaring away every peccary with functioning ears for miles around. Bolivar gave me a disgusted look just before leading us on another short sprint. We stopped again, and again I coughed idiotically, but by this point it didn't seem to matter because we were so close that even *I* could smell the peccaries. It was a thick, mildly unpleasant scent that filled my nose, a muskiness mingled with what vaguely resembled the pungent bite of human body odor.

We were moving again, this time through thick mud. Bolivar and Elias, shotguns drawn, were running in a crouch, so I did the same. I could hear animal grunts up ahead now, and when I looked I saw pig figures flashing and scrambling, running away. Bolivar turned sharply to the left and disappeared at the same moment Elias stopped, stood, aimed, and fired. The explosion reverberated through the forest, drawing shrieks from a group of parrots overhead. I followed Elias forward to a downed peccary weighing at least eighty pounds. It lay on its side, rear legs twitching violently from a bleeding, mortal wound to the head. Its cylindrical black snout was stained red with blood just above its long, curving yellow tusks.

Panting from the run, my chest heaving, I took in the sight while Elias grabbed a long, thin branch from a nearby palm. He jammed the branch into his shotgun muzzle, ejecting the spent shell from the breach end of the barrel—a necessity with this simple model. He reloaded, but by now the rest of the peccaries were gone—as was Bolivar, who was in hot pursuit.

Elias and Norma busied themselves gathering vines of varying widths and lengths to tie the now motionless pig into a crescent shape, a hind leg threaded through the tied-shut jaws. A thicker vine rose from either end of this arrangement and formed a U that served as a sort of carrying handle or sling. This allowed the peccary to be carried on Elias' back, anchored by the vine sling which would be looped over his head to come to rest across the front of his front shoulders.

As the peccary was being so prepared, another shotgun blast sounded a short distance away. Bolivar had finally drawn a bead on others in the pack. We set off in that direction as a second shot boomed, then a third—and by the time we arrived, three peccaries lay dead at Bolivar's feet, victims of flawless marksmanship. While they collected more vines for transport, all three Indians burst into their native Cofan, reliving the hunt several times over with descriptive hand gestures and theatrical speech—the benedictory habit of successful hunters everywhere.

It was probably just as well I couldn't understand the particulars of what was being said. My brain was elsewhere, already focused on the disturbing arithmetic and geography of our situation. With his deadly aim, Bolivar had dropped two adult peccaries indistinguishable in size from Elias's—about eighty pounds—plus an offspring caught in the melee weighing roughly fifteen pounds, a poodle-sized runt. So there we were with our game more than a mile, it turned out, from the river. In all, there were four of us human beings, three men and a woman. And there were four peccaries, three adults and a poodle-size pip-squeak baby.

Peccary Hunting in the Amazon

In one respect, the Cofan were different from most of the traditional peoples I had visited in my life. Women were not exploited as de facto mules, routinely given the hardest physical labor as in, say, most of Africa. Cofan men tended to share in the heaviest lifting, the toughest grunt work. More than this, though, it was my own vanity, my own old-fashioned or New Age (take your pick) sense that a man was a man with certain responsibilities no matter what the culture or situation, that led me to reject two possibilities. I would not watch Norma moan under the heft of a brawny adult peccary while I skipped to the river with the lithe poodle dangling around my neck. Nor would I abide the sight of Bolivar or Elias making two trips in order to transport all three adult peccaries between the two of them.

That left one option.

"I'll carry a big one," I told Bolivar. "Give it to me."

The same question had been on his mind, I could tell, as he finished tying up the last peccary. Both he and Elias had been casting speculative glances my way in an apparent effort to assess my mettle. Was the gringo going to resolve this awkward situation with honor? their eyes seemed to ask.

"It's very heavy, Mike," Bolivar said, skepticism in his voice. "Are you sure you want it?"

"Give it to me," I repeated.

Bolivar lifted one of the peccaries and I slipped my head through the vine loop, the vine itself coming to rest across my chest and around my shoulders. When he let go completely, I grew very confused. It was an eerie shock to feel the warmth of the peccary's body heat, not yet diminished, spreading across my back. But it was the weight, the astonishing leaden load suddenly resting on my spine, that made me think for a moment that Bolivar, too, was piggybacking atop my frame as a prank. When I swung slowly around, however, and saw Bolivar standing five paces off, staring back at me with a look of deep concern, I knew I was in a fix of Mayday proportions.

The problem wasn't the weight alone—though the weight *was* like carrying a small person on my back. The problem was just as much the technique. I could already feel the anchoring front vine of this minimalist Indian backpack digging sharply into my shoulders. The vine had a discomfiting straightjacket effect, lashing my upper arms like cement to my torso, leaving the limbs all but useless for maintaining balance. I found that in order to walk at all I had to lace my thumbs through the front of the vine and lean significantly forward. But then the awkward shape of the peccary itself came into play, the contours of whose skull I could feel in painful profile against my upper back.

Carrying so much weight in such a fashion for more than a mile might have been a survivable ordeal had the land before us been flat, dry, and unobstructed. But of course it was none of these. All I had to do was walk one hundred feet with the peccary—struggling in a waddling fashion through thick mud and around a fallen tree—and I knew I'd never make it even halfway to the river. I knew it.

But I tried. I put one foot in front of the other and followed Bolivar, Elias, and Norma to the last stream we had crossed. There, despite their own charges, the Indians tightroped along the same narrow log as before. Then I crossed my way. Without the use of my arms, I somehow slid down the bank to the stream and entered the water. Wading through, though, the mud was so thick that my left foot, with a protracted sucking sound, came sliding completely out of my boot. The boot itself remained mired in the gook. Bolivar had to retrieve it and put it back on my foot for me when—by some miracle—I made it to the top of the far bank on my own.

Everything became a blur after these ugly opening moves. It was a strange slow-motion torture of forward movement full of blood, sweat, and mosquitoes, of long waddles through stagnant swamps, of tricky footing on strained knees, of almost, almost, almost falling with every tenth step. I slipped badly coming out of the next stream and only at the last second freed my thumb from under the straightjacket vine in time to grab the closest tree to steady myself. But the narrow trunk I reached for was a peculiar species of palm with needlelike thorns protruding thick as hair from its bark. Bolivar turned around just in time to see me pulling three of the thorns from my palm with my teeth—and I realized I was embarrassing myself more with this mammoth adult on my back than if I'd carried the poodle.

Bolivar couldn't have agreed more, I'm sure, though he was trying to be delicate.

"Just put it down," he kept saying, only a soupçon of scorn in his voice. "It's heavy. Let my wife carry it for a while. It's okay."

But idiotically, the weaker I became from the beating and the fatigue of the march, the more obsessed I grew with making it to the river. I've long since given up trying to explain it, for the drive far outstripped any western sense of finish-what-you-start Puritanism. Some schmo in a lab coat might have honed in on an inordinate fear of failure—and be close to the mark. But whatever the case, my thinking grew as piggish as the meat on my back: I *had* to reach the canoe with this lashed-on cargo or I'd never be able to face myself in the mirror reflection of the Zabalo River again.

"I'll make it," I kept telling Bolivar after each of his appeals. "I'll make it."

But to continue trying I had to resort to an even slower pace, a walking crawl, really. Elias and Norma broke off for the river, leaving Bolivar behind to tend to me. Every time I looked up he was standing still, waiting for me. He was barely stooped under the weight of his own pig, his taut body a work of steel that silently mocked the wreck of my own arms and legs. I began resting every fifty yards now, discovering that if I stopped and bent far forward I could table the peccary on my back, relieving the pressure on my shoulders and neck. As for the carrying vine across my front shoulders that was now digging and scraping into my skin to the point of drawing blood, I tried padding it by stuffing copious amounts of leaves between it and my flesh. That this didn't help wasn't important after a while when the entire area became utterly numb. I lost all sensation across my shoulders.

I'm not sure how I made the last quarter mile. We entered the dense, dark stretch of trees where mosquitoes attacked us mercilessly. With my arms immobilized by the vine, I could do little to swat the insects away. Nor could I reach up and remove my glasses when they again fogged to uselessness. Bolivar removed the glasses for me, an act which dramatically reduced my ability to see the approach of face-level branches and other nuisances. My head became a punching bag.

In the deep mud of the next creek bed I lost my boot a second time. I pulled myself out of the creek with enormous effort, one foot exposed, and called up to Bolivar. He turned and stared—and despite obvious effort he couldn't stifle a laugh at the humpbacked, mud-spattered, half-blind gringo covered with mosquitoes limping toward him with just one boot on, cursing a wild streak of English bad words. It was my rock-bottom bottom. I didn't try to hide it. Bolivar went back to fetch the boot, still chuckling to himself, while I paused to table the peccary on my back for a breather.

And that's when I quit. I tossed in the towel—finally. This was preposterous, I realized. I was faint with exhaustion, close to collapse. What exactly was the point?

I was just about to sling the lead-weight peccary onto the ground when, still hunched over, I saw two muddy feet step into my frame of vision. They were Elias's feet. He had reached the river, deposited his peccary in the canoe, and come back.

"How far is it?" I asked him, still staring at his feet, unable to stand just yet.

"Close," he said. "Give me your animal."

Somehow I straightened my spine. Still carrying the pig, I stepped back into the boot Bolivar was now holding for me like Cinderella's royal suitor.

"I'll make it," I said. "I want to make it."

Bolivar grimaced. "But Mike, you can't . . ."

I started walking.

Cruelly, just as victory seemed nearest, the pain was greatest, cracking out all over my body during those last few stubborn steps. Up ahead, I could see a clearing. It was getting closer, bigger. There was more sunlight. Then the river was before me, down one last sloping bank which I negotiated in one last rump slide, reaching the beached canoe. I maneuvered my fanny to a gunwale, wobbled slightly, and then unloaded my charge in a loud thunk to the canoe floor. I then made my own thunk on the sandy shore, lying on my back, limp with relief, smiling despite the lingering hurt. I was too spent to whoop or otherwise vocalize the fact that, inwardly, my soul was doing a pirouette of utter joy against a backdrop of happy, booming fireworks.

I looked up and saw Bolivar and Elias bending over me, silhouetted against the sky, grinning down at me.

"*Gracias*," Bolivar said. "*Muchas gracias*, Mike. Muchas gracias for carrying the pig."

"*De nada*," I managed.

"Rest now," he said. "Rest a long time. It's okay."

"I'm not a Cofan," I whispered back.

The men were still peering down, straining to hear. "What?" they said.

"I'm not a Cofan," I repeated.

They heard me clearly this time, but were no less baffled.

"What I mean," I said, still breathing hard, "is I don't know how you do these things. I'm not a Cofan. I almost died carrying that pig."

My comments struck them as absolutely hilarious for some reason and the men laughed uncontrollably, and for the rest of the day they kept asking me, "Mike, are you a Cofan?" and I'd say "no" and they'd laugh some more.

We all rested there on the riverbank for a while, reposing long enough to face up to the implacable fact: We were still a long way from the village without a motor and now with 250 pounds of added peccary meat to contend with.

It was well past sunset when we finally pulled up to the huts, tired and hungry. We'd been caught in a heavy rainstorm along the way and our hair and clothes were miserably wet. I was shivering uncontrollably.

Bolivar's oldest son came to greet us on the riverbank to help carry gear.

"Come take the backpack of this Cofan man," Bolivar said to his son while gesturing toward me. His son was confused. "Carry this Cofan man's *bag*," Bolivar repeated with some sharpness. I managed to produce an exhausted smile— as did Bolivar and Elias and Norma, as his son finally reached for my gear.

V
Planes, Trains, Cars

15
John T. Love and the Flight from Hell

To say the plane was experiencing turbulence is like saying Michael Jordan can shoot an okay game of hoop. In the wordless passenger cabin (*nobody* talks when it's this bad) the truth pressed against every mind like the sharp edge of a black box: Some force other than the pilot was in complete control of this twin-propeller, thirty-four-seat, Saab 340.

Think free-falling piano. Think runaway elevator. That's what the vertical drops were like. And the terrible uplifts! Each was an Apollo blastoff in miniature. But the worst of it, by far, was the fierce sliding from side to side. The plane seemed to be on a sheet of freshly Zamboni'd ice, whipsawed wildly for interminable distances to starboard, to port.

And mind you, I'm no virgin. I've flown all over the world on airlines you've never heard of—Kyrgyz Air, Air Zaire—and some, shudder, you have:

Aeroflot, Valu-Jet. I once was in a rickety C-130 lost over the Amazon jungle in a terrifying, heavy fog. Another time, I watched horror-stricken as my flight from Cairo jettisoned its fuel over the Mediterranean in preparation for "an unscheduled landing due to technical reasons" in Crete. With engines failing, the pilot somehow made a perfect, successful landing on a tarmac crowded with waiting fire trucks.

Yet as extreme as these events may seem, none comes close to the flight at hand: a late-night, 230-mile, New York–to–Washington shuttle flight caught in the violent maw of an amazing band of late-spring thunderstorms. With lightning flashing outside the windows like exploding bombs, illuminating the screaming, rain-pelted propellers, the pilot twice attempted to communicate with us. But no one knew what he was trying to say because five words into each message, the plane would do another piano plummet and the microphone would cut off. Just like that. In mid-sentence. Did the pilot just have a heart attack? Was he gripping cockpit controls gone suddenly haywire, yelling "Mayday! Mayday!" to some unreachable airport? We didn't know. Twice this happened.

Still worse, I hate to fly. Even under perfect weather conditions I'm a certified airplane-phobe, a minor wreck. It's odd, but what's happening now is utterly familiar to me because I've dreamed it all before in a thousand nightmares. Only this time it really *is* happening. I rolled up an inflight magazine and began banging it against my head while loudly, absurdly, spontaneously humming, "Mary Had a Little Lamb" to try to drown out the roaring propellers and all those thoughts of impending, fiery ka-boom.

Just then, a poor, sick passenger in front of me somehow made his way to the plane's sole bathroom only to have a particularly violent wind surge throw him against the door, breaking the lock, and leaving him banging to get out. While the lone flight attendant went to help, unbuckling herself at the risk of broken bones, I kept banging my head with the magazine, eyes shut against the flashing lightning, humming my nursery rhyme. And that's when I heard the voice.

John T. Love and the Flight from Hell

"What's your name?" the voice asked. The question was repeated several times before I looked over at the perfectly calm African-American man in his fifties seated next to me. He was a big man with a face rugged and weathered like a sailor's and preposterously serene. His hand, sans a single tremble, was outstretched. "Shake my hand," he said. "Shake my hand."

Finally, I did.

"My name," the man said, "is John T. Love. And I think I can help you."

In a situation where I needed a miracle to survive, one had arrived. Some god somewhere had heard my prayers and had sent me his love, two hundred pounds of it. It completely filled the seat next to me: John T. Love, retired U.S. Marine Corps sergeant, rescuer of a babbling, ghost-white stranger in complete coach-class meltdown: me.

In George Orwell's novel *1984*, the state is able to read minds and give people the exact punishment they secretly fear most. The book's protagonist is thus forced to endure an attack by rats from his neck up. I don't mean to exaggerate, but for people who really, *really* hate to get on airplanes—like me—the act of flying comes close to Orwell's imagined punishment. Worse, in my own case, some dark force in the universe has read my mind and given me a job where I have to fly a lot.

My fear of flying is not rational—no phobias are—so it stubbornly refuses to lessen even after innumerable flights in my thirty-eight years. I've adopted all manner of pathetic superstitions, of course, like briefly sitting on all my luggage for good luck before each flight. Yet I'm still known to grab the hand of a complete stranger and squeeze for all I'm worth during the most routine, eventless takeoff.

Two things, however, have carried me through all those tens of thousands of miles through airports as chaotic as Moscow's domestic terminal and as obscure as the tiny Bahamian airstrip called Dead Man's Cay. They are, in order of importance: lots of airport beer and the firm assumption that all is not lost—no matter what my phobia tells me—until the flight attendants begin to

173

look genuinely concerned. And the latter, as everyone knows, almost never, ever happens.

So you can imagine the horror—the *horror!*—when the sole flight attendant on this pummeled Saab 340 flight got on her cabin microphone and, with the plane again in total free fall, declared that she was essentially too terrified to get out of her seat. From my aisle slot (*never* sit by a window), I glanced furtively back at the attendant. Her seat was against the cabin's back wall, and she had strapped herself in with double seat belts that crossed against her chest like bandoleers. After heroically breaking down the bathroom door to free the trapped passenger, the attendant looked somewhat drained of blood, especially in the knuckle area, and she was having trouble speaking. "Please," she announced, "nobody . . . leave . . . their seats. If you do, there's nothing . . . I can do . . . to help you."

I would have traded places with anyone in the world not inside this plane. And at that very moment, unbeknownst to me, a friend of mine was far, far below, driving her pickup truck along I-95 from Baltimore, Maryland, to Washington, D.C. She later told me surface winds nearly blew her truck off the highway. She had to struggle with the steering wheel just to stay on the road. And the rain! What blinding rain! When I told her I was on a plane from New York that night, she stopped me cold, in midsentence, and said, "Oh my *God!* You mean you were up in the *sky* that night? You were up in *that!* Oh my God!"

Just then, the plane went into another neck-jarring slide, a careening motion to the right that went on and on. And on and on. How far could it go? Even in my state of paralyzing fear, part of me managed a flash of sick fascination for the sheer physics of all this. On and on and on. It was supernatural.

By now I had completely zoned out John T. Love, the kind-faced passenger next to me who had introduced himself. I was humming and banging my head again, sinking back into my own dark place when his hand seized my magazine in midstroke, stopping me cold.

"I *said*," he half yelled just inches from my face, "what seems to be the problem?"

John T. Love and the Flight from Hell

I realized then that I wasn't the craziest person on the plane.

I answered sarcastically, "What seems to be the *problem?* We're all going to *die!* That's what. Just look at the flight attendant. Look at her! And that guy in the bathroom. Did you see that?"

"I saw it," said Love. "And I'm telling you, we're not going to die. Get that out of your head. In fact, this flight—"

An Apollo liftoff threw us back against our seats, pinning us there, ending all conversation. Up, up, up we went. Then, savagely, there was a wild slide to port followed by an abrupt free fall. I felt myself coming out of my chair, literally levitating, held in only by my overworked seatbelt.

"Like I was saying," Love continued once we'd stabilized enough to catch a breath. "This flight is nothing. This is chump change. I was a marine my whole career. Lots of low-altitude flights in terrible weather—in training and combat. This flight is chump change."

Yeah? I thought. Well I've ridden tin pot, Soviet-made Yak 40s in Central Asia through notoriously unstable air above Himalayan foothills. I once took a Vietnam Airlines flight over the Gulf of Tonkin in winds approaching monsoon force. *Those* flights were chump change. *This* flight . . . this was the gold standard of turbulence. I don't care if you've been to the *moon* on a harried marine transport plane.

I would have told Love all this but for one problem: I literally couldn't speak any more. Maybe it was the sound of the broken bathroom door banging open and shut, its hinges and handle destroyed, that finally did it. Or maybe it was the luggage bin that had suddenly opened during the last free fall, allowing airplane pillows and blankets to spill shockingly into the aisle, unretrieved. Whatever the trigger, I was done for now, a mute.

The pilot, it turned out, was trying different headings and altitudes every few minutes, frantically attempting to escape the ferocious winds—to no avail. Each change brought another sledgehammer blow. We were trapped in an unusually long and wide squall line of thunderstorms violently engulfing the whole upper East Coast. To this day I wonder why the pilot didn't just land the plane at the nearest airport. But perhaps even this too was dangerous. I imagined a chorus of air traffic controllers up and down the East Coast yelling into headset mikes: "Not here! Not here! We've closed the airport! The heavens are falling. Stay away!"

Love clearly saw me slipping into my air-commuter coma, because he became even more insistent on talking to me. He turned and faced me squarely, giving me the look of a sergeant addressing a grunt unable to move a muscle during an awful firefight. The look was one of impatience, urgency, mild contempt, and yet knowing sympathy.

"Have you ever been in the military, son?" Love asked, staring directly into my fear-sodden eyes.

I said nothing.

"*Answer,* son!"

I finally shook my head, just barely comprehending.

"No? Okay," Love said. "Hmmm. We'll have to try another route."

I raised my magazine, ready to start head banging again, when Love said, "As a kid, did you ever go to amusement parks for fun? Did you ever ride the rides at amusement parks?"

Again I couldn't speak, but finally—after Love asked several more times—I nodded my head yes.

"Yes! Of course you did!" Love said. "And I bet I know what your favorite ride was. Come on. Tell me. What was your favorite ride?"

Though clearly a nice guy, Love was now becoming an irritant. These childish matters distracted me from my adult responsibility to panic deeply. Even in my clouded state, I could see where he was going with this—and I just didn't have time.

"Come on. What was your favorite ride?"

I couldn't just nod or shake my head this time, and Love was insisting I speak. To shut him up and get back to my maniacal humming, I summoned all my strength and let my lips form the words: "Roll-er coast-er."

John T. Love and the Flight from Hell

"Exactly!" Love exclaimed. "You rode roller coasters! Exactly! Don't you see? That's all this plane is. It's a roller coaster."

That's supposed to help me? I thought. But before I could roll my eyes he said something that got my full and undivided attention.

"This turbulence we're experiencing now is not here to scare us or to hurt us. This turbulence is here for our *pleasure*."

What gall! What hubris! Love wasn't just tweaking the noses of the storm gods with such blasphemy. He was rearranging their faces entirely. As if I didn't have enough to worry about, I now wanted this man as far away from me as possible, certain that the next bolt of lightning was going to crash through the window and strike him dead.

For the third and final time, the cockpit pilot switched on the cabin intercom and tried to talk to us. He sounded terrible, as exhausted and rattled as the blond flight attendant still seated behind us, still rigidly grasping her seatbelt bandoleers and looking tragically underpaid, hanging on like the rest of us. "Ladies and gentlemen," the pilot said as more airplane pillows tumbled from the overhead bin. "Please try not to worry. But we just can't seem to get—"

Piannnnooooooooooooooooo plummet!!!! It was ugly, this one—and the moment it started the pilot once again was cut off in midsentence. Two different passengers in rows toward the front spontaneously shouted out to the pilot: "*Don't* talk to us! *Don't* talk! Just fly the plane! Just fly!"

"Let me ask you something," Love went on, not missing a beat, amazingly oblivious to everything around him, calm as a Buddhist monk in meditation. "When you rode those roller coasters as a kid, where did you sit?"

I was still reeling from the pilot's failed communique. How could a flight be this bad? How could the pilot be so engaged in just keeping us airborne that he couldn't press a microphone button and utter a handful of complete sentences?

"Come *onnnnnn!*" Love said. "You know where the best seat on the roller coaster was. Where did you always like to sit?"

I decided to answer the lunatic's questions as quickly as possible now, trying to get this exchange over with so I could hunker back down to serious freak-out mode.

"The last seat!" I blurted out. "The best seats were always toward the rear."

"Exactly," Love said. "Exactly. The seats at the back got the most action, like the end of a whip, moving all over the place. And look!" he continued. "That's where we're sitting. Almost at the rear of this plane. We've got excellent roller coaster seats, don't you think?"

How much crazier could this get? Yes, we were on the eleventh of fourteen cabin rows. So what? Wherever Love was trying to take me, it wasn't helping. He had gone from irritant to full-blown nuisance.

"I've got one last question," he said, apparently reading my mind. "Then I promise I'll leave you alone. When you rode all those roller coasters as a kid, sitting in those backseats, there was one other thing you did to make the ride even better, to make it the most fun ride it could possibly be. What was that thing you did? You know what it was."

I was finished with Love. I didn't have time. We were back on the just-Zamboni'd ice, tearing through a heart-stopping slide to the left. On and on, it went. I couldn't have talked even if I wanted to.

But Love could. "What was that thing you would do?" he pressed me as we both leaned to the right, me into him, he into the fuselage wall. He managed to fight the Gs enough to turn his face back toward me. "What was that thing you used to do on the roller coaster? You *know* what it was. Come on. Tell me!"

I somehow managed as the slide went on. "I . . . put . . . my . . . arms . . . up . . . in . . . the . . . air," I said. "I waved . . . my arms . . . above my head. O . . . *kay?*"

"*Exactly!*" Love said. "That's it! That's what you did." After the briefest of pauses in which the plane's slide came to a jerking stop, only to begin a forward free fall, Love said, "So come on, let's do it! Let's do it!"

Next there came only silence from his direction. He had stopped talking to me, and by the time I looked over, his arms were already up in the air. With the plane falling forward like a big, arcing bomb heading for a collision with Earth, Love had his arms up in the air and was wildly leaning into the fall. His look had all the weird exuberance of the warhead bronco-riding scene from Dr. Strangelove.

"Yeeeee-hawww!" Love yelled. "Come on! Get 'em up! Get 'em up! Get your hands up. It's roller coaster time!"

I realized then that to save the plane, to rescue all the passengers and myself, I had to stop this man. He was taunting fate, a disaster magnet. Several saucer-eyed passengers glanced back to investigate the commotion. Seeing Love, arms up as if in surrender, they turned back around, confused and more terrified.

"Get 'em up!" Love yelled out to me. "Get 'em up!"

Only the acute desire to save my life from this terrorism gave me the energy to begin lifting my arms. If I put my arms up briefly and reported how little it helped me, perhaps he would scuttle the idea.

With my rolled-up inflight magazine still in my hand, I lifted my arms slowly, overcoming in a few seconds a whole mountain of fear. To emerge from a hunkered down, cowering position during intense turbulence and to lift your arms into the air, holding onto nothing, is for an airplane phobe the ultimate act of letting go, pure and simple. It's bungee jumping the Grand Canyon without the bungee part. When my hands reached shoulder height, Love said, "That's it! That's it! You can do it! Keep going."

When my arms reached the full outstretched position, fingers splayed just below the ceiling, Love didn't say anything. He just looked at me, his head bobbing from the constant turbulence, his own arms still in the air, and smiled.

Because he knew.

My fear had vanished.

We were in another piano drop when this happened. Down, down, down we went before switching back to blastoff mode—up, up, up. I had to struggle to keep my arms in the air during the liftoff part, but I made sure to do it because . . . *it felt so good!*

"Wheewww! That was a good one," Love said, after the plane had stablized.

He looked at me and I at him in a moment of insane and resplendent poignancy. The retired marine corps sergeant and combat veteran facing the candy-ass thirtysomething journalist, our arms up in the air like bank tellers in a robbery, chatting with each other. "I can't believe how . . . *relieved* I feel," I said.

"I know," he said. "Isn't it great?"

More passengers began looking over their shoulders at the spectacle, their eyes full of heightened panic. I think they thought we were reaching for oxygen masks or something because several began looking up at their own ceiling space, trying to figure out what to do.

We began a terrible slide to the right, causing Love's and my arms to sway mightily and in unison to the left. I laughed—a laugh!—at the sudden thought that we looked like two men doing the wave at a college football game. Next, a headwind blast sent us forward, and one of my hands brushed against the head of the woman in front of me. She turned, gasping. "I'm so sorry," I said, adding, "Hey, if you lift your arms it really helps." But she didn't do it.

"Oh, that was a good one," I said to Love after the next particularly good blastoff. It really did feel like a roller coaster. We spent the last forty-five minutes of the flight this way, lowering our arms during brief lulls, then raising them again to enjoy the full fun of more appalling, outlandish rockiness.

Why did raising our arms help? I spent a lot of time thinking about it afterwards, and I believe that rigidly hunkering down during turbulence only amplifies the wild movement of the plane; but freely letting yourself be a part of the motion reduces the impact physically while simultaneously taming somehow the monster in your mind. Once you yield, in a sense, you're no longer in mortal combat.

After a very bumpy landing in Washington, John T. Love and I made haste for the door with the other exhausted passengers. We had to walk across the tarmac to our gate and I remember hearing an American flag snapping violently in the stiff wind—*pop! pop! pop!* It was absurdly warm, eerily warm, for early May around midnight. It was, I knew, classic tornado weather. I looked back at the plane, so small and vulnerable, propellers winding down. It looked bruised somehow from all the pummeling. Despite Love's wonderful coping mechanism, the plane's fragility reaffirmed my belief that we're not supposed to be up there. If we were meant to fly, we'd all have wings. Period. It's totally Promethean: We've stolen something and the gods are pissed. Tonight I'd simply been spared.

At baggage claim, while everyone talked nonstop about the flight, I turned to Love and thanked him over and over again. I assumed he had developed this high-altitude skill over decades of accompanying greenhorn marines up into foul weather. As for me, I've not seen turbulence like that since, though during the normal bumps and drops of plane trips I still flash my arms into the air to keep my skills up.

Love's bags came first. I'd just shared one of the most intense experiences of my life with him and I didn't know what to say. I gave him my card, but he didn't offer his. He was visiting a daughter in Washington, he said. "Maybe I'll see you on another flight some day," he said.

And then, just like that, he was gone, vanishing into the windy night. Flying away like an angel.

Of love.

16

Old Ghosts on a
Southern Highway

Things are not entirely what they seem along the Natchez Trace Parkway, a two-lane highway that wends its leisurely way for 450 miles—between Nashville, Tennessee, and Natchez, Mississippi— through a multi-chaptered panorama of the deep and grand South. The road knits a region of ghosts and witches, fiery preachers and temples built to ancient gods. Call it the spiritual province. I'm not immune to its pull. I'm a native southerner, with Choctaw Indian blood on one side of my family and a Civil War veteran from Mississippi on the other. For me, a trip here is a journey home.

From leafy Appalachian foothills to cypress swamps hung with Spanish moss, the Natchez Trace is so powerfully beautiful that the ancient Choctaw deemed part of this region their promised land. But behind the natural beauty that graces every bend in the road lies a rich human history laced with tales both tall and small.

The Trace most likely began as a wilderness footpath used by Indian hunters. By the late 1700s it was a way home for Mississippi River flatboatmen; then it was a mail road, a military road, and finally an abandoned road. The Natchez Trace of today, resurrected in the 1930s by the National Park Service, runs through a conservative region, rough-hewn in character, backwoods in feel, where relics of the past mingle with walking, talking relics of the present.

I encounter Wilburn Stagges, a retired cotton farmer and active squirrel-dog keeper, on the first afternoon of my four-day drive. We meet up just past the grave site of Meriwether Lewis, who, back in the early 1800s, made an ill-fated detour onto the Trace on his way from St. Louis to Washington, D.C.

Stagges, thumbs hooked in his overalls, tries to convince me to buy one of his dogs. It's a mutt used for hunting the squirrels people around here still eat. "They're good with turnip greens," Stagges says. I decline the dog, and we start talking about Meriwether Lewis. In 1809 Lewis suffered two fatal gun-shot wounds inside an inn near present-day Hohenwald, Tennessee. It's still a mystery who fired the gun—some think Lewis was murdered, some think it was suicide, some think he shot himself by accident.

"I'll tell you this, though," says Stagges, "most people around here don't think Lewis should be dug up. Leave the man's bones alone." Stagges is refer-ring to the modern forensic gumshoes who would like to solve the Lewis rid-dle with a little spadework. For the present, anyway, the mystery remains.

I awake my second day in Florence, Alabama, a drowsy little city on a curve of the Tennessee River. I promptly head toward the river, then climb seventy-two steps to the top of the steep-sided Wawmanona Indian Mound. Here in Florence, as elsewhere along the Trace, Native American roots stretch back to the mist of prehistory.

"Some people still see this place as holy," says Jack Parkhurst, the silver-haired septuagenarian keeper of the two-thousand-year-old mound. We're both breathing hard from the climb up to the top. It's a warm late-winter day and we're forty-two feet up in the sky, on the mound summit, the Tennessee River glimmering below us. "We don't know who these Indians were," Parkhurst says. "But we know this was a place for worship, not burial."

He adds that a special arbor, called the Tree of Heaven, grows wild along the mound's edge. I can feel the tug of holiness below my feet. Just then, in a flash, I see my first robin of the year fly directly overhead.

I feel lucky as I drive farther south, wending through the rural Alabama landscape. I pass brightly named places like Freedom Hills and a road called Friendship. I see white-tailed deer darting through last year's cotton fields, with fluffy unpicked bolls lying atop the black earth like forgotten pearls.

As soon as I enter Mississippi I feel a surge of nostalgia. Near Baldwyn I relive a boyhood ritual, exiting the Trace for a moon pie and RC Cola at an old general store with a moss-speckled tin roof.

As I head back, driving below the boughs of century-old oak trees, a sign catches my eye: Spring Hill Missionary Baptist Church: Founded 1800. Curious, I knock on the church door and meet the African-American Reverend Allen Watson, Jr. With four of his twelve children, Watson is busily preparing the small sanctuary for an old-fashioned three-day revival which will begin later that night. The church was founded by slaves in 1800 when this part of northern Mississippi was home to Chickasaw Indians and a few struggling pioneer farms scattered along the old Natchez Trace.

"We still sing some of the old slave songs," says Watson. "Like, 'I'm Waiting on You Lord.' That song's not written down anywhere. It's in none of the hymnals. It's handed down."

At Watson's invitation, I return that night for the start of the revival. The twenty pinewood pews are packed, with the choir swinging and swaying, all arms uplifted. The visiting evangelist, a young preacher from Illinois, is late. When he finally arrives, he explains that a miracle has happened. Just a few miles from the church, he was in an accident and his car was totaled.

"The windshield came crashing down against my face," he says, turning his cheek to the congregation. "But look, God's merciful hand has shielded me. Not one cut. Not one abrasion."

Awestruck, the congregation lets fly with "amens" and "hallelujahs," and the revival is off to a foot-stompin' roar that goes on well into the night.

My spirit sanctified, I continue south the next morning. I pass Tupelo, Mississippi, that muse to a thousand southern poets with its giant magnolias and porch fronts lined with white, fluted columns. Gradually, the land turns flatter. Tall pines mix with graceful ash, chestnut oak, and beech trees all around—and patches of swampland begin to brush up against the parkway. North of Houston, Mississippi, I stop to read a historic marker titled Witch Dance. According to local folklore, this spot was a meeting place for witches in pioneer days. Wherever the witches stepped, grass won't grow even today, the myth goes.

I spy a nearby Park Service groundskeeper and ask him about the witch business. He becomes a bit more serious than I'd like. "Two things," he says. "Three years ago, this here rest room building burned down. We never learned who did it. And see that sign over there?" He walks me back to the historic marker. There's patchy grass below. "See these bald spots? I've put fertilizer here. I've put seed here. And grass won't grow. Never." He smiles ambiguously, and I slip back into my car, smiling back, not sure what to believe.

Fifty miles farther down the road, in the tiny town of French Camp, I devour a steaming plate of bread pudding inside a 171-year-old log cabin cafe. Don Smith, the cook, tells me the town's central feature is a 1,200-acre farm and school for orphaned and disadvantaged kids. The students feed horses and tend cornfields before class in the cathartic rural calm along the modern Trace parkway. "It's amazing how that kind of life can turn a troubled city kid around," says Smith. "That—and a lot of love from teachers."

Here, I realize, miracles happen every day.

I spend the night at the Redbud Inn, just a skip down the Trace in Kosciusko, Mississippi, near the narrow and brooding Yockanookany River. The South is full of tales of haunted mansions, so I'm not especially surprised when Maggie Garrett, owner of this rambling, gingerbread, 114-year-old Queen Anne Victorian inn, warns me about Miss Lillie, the inn's "friendly" ghost. The ghost isn't noisy, Garrett says, but she might rearrange my things or entice me with her fragrant perfume. I smile appreciatively, knowing my leg's being yanked.

But around one o'clock I awake to a sound similar to a wetted finger moving along the rim of a crystal glass. It's a beautiful, eerie, high-pitched humming tone. It's coming from directly above my bed. It stops only to return an hour later, which is when I feel a stir of fright. Then I smell it: a fragrance less like perfume than the smell of a sweet liquor combined with a sharp herbal spice I can't quite place. If this is a ghost, I decide, friendly or not, she's been drinking. I sleep fitfully the rest of the night.

I'm happy to hit the road the next day, driving the final miles of the Trace parkway, deep in Mississippi. Sylvan swampland decorates the way with graceful gray herons and bald cypresses mirrored in tea-colored water.

The town of Natchez, on the Mississippi River, is the end of the line. I arrive at the start of the city's celebrated Spring Pilgrimage, a festival where guests can journey back in time by touring antebellum homes and attending events such as a Confederate pageant and a gospel choir. I wander through a few well-appointed plantation homes, each featuring a female guide in hoopskirt, then I duck into a bar right on the Mississippi River.

Thirsty and pleasantly tired from the rich journey that began in Tennessee four days before, I decide to indulge in that most southern of southern clichés. Kenny the bartender brings me an ice-cold mint julep, his own special mix of Southern Comfort, mint water, shaved ice, and sugar in a highball glass. I take a sip, lean back on my bar stool, and decide I've just tasted home. Then I decide something else: It was mint. I smelled mint the other night at that haunted inn. Miss Lillie, the ghost, had been drinking mint juleps.

Of course.

17
Relic Hunting on a Pioneer Trail

S omething catches my eye that first afternoon along a winsome stretch of rural road just outside West Friendship, Maryland, in Howard County. It's more than just the wood-shingled log cabin that appears to be at least 175 years old. It's the cabin door. It's just three-and-a-half feet high. It looks absurd. Why so short?

I knock at the old yellow farmhouse next to the empty cabin for an answer. No response. I holler inside a red-roofed barn out back, and only a cat meows from atop a rusty pile of tools. I stick my head inside a series of rambling greenhouses strewn across the back field of this working farm and finally find owner Joe Festerling. He's a German immigrant with a pronounced accent and he's rearranging a forest of flourishing begonias.

"The cabin door?" he says in the German accent that renders the word "the" as "zee." He wipes black soil from his hands and leads me back to the roadside cabin. "The door was for the thieves, you know."

It's day one of my self-declared mission: to traverse nearly the entire state of Maryland along an all-but-forgotten relic called the National Road, one of America's oldest and most fabled pioneer trails west. Built between 1811 and 1852 along a course that would later become (mostly) two-lane U.S. Route 40, the National Road was a turnpike spanning 750 miles from the Chesapeake Bay to Vandalia, Illinois. It crossed a middle passage of the Appalachian Mountains and so opened the fertile Midwest to settlers. I'm exploring the trail's two-hundred-mile Maryland segment, from the sea-level flatness of Baltimore's Lombard Street to the ear-popping mountains of Maryland's western panhandle.

And I'm getting my first extended history lesson. According to farmer Festerling, this particular cabin was built to house workers constructing the National Road through Howard County. The door was made barely three-and-a-half feet high so that the highway thieves and other rascals of that frontier period would have to crouch low to enter, a disorienting procedure that gave people inside the chance to wallop them over the head.

"Very clever, don't you think?" says Festerling, simulating a chop to his forehead.

As Festerling speaks, time's curtains seem to part and I fall through. It's not just the obvious authenticity of the cabin, with its flat-sided logs "chinked" together with stones in the pioneer style. Nor is it the treasury of nineteenth-century "trail" artifacts that Festerling has collected behind the cabin, including an 1840 Conestoga wagon jack made entirely of hand-forged iron.

It's the man's accent. German pioneers settled all along the National Road in Howard and Frederick counties in the nineteenth century, and Festerling has followed suit, drawn to America's open spaces like his ancestors, turning the soil along this surviving ribbon of roadway history.

Relic Hunting on a Pioneer Trail

So when he drops to one knee to show me how the wagon jack works with his dirt-stained hands, and as his German "zees" and "zats" fly through the air, I might as well be back on the original road. I can almost hear the rattle of stagecoaches and see the buckskin-clad pioneers who, at the National Road's peak around 1840, traveled west by the tens of thousands, toting guns and axle grease and leading herds of cattle.

Remarkably, this time travel feeling occurs numerous times during my three-day journey across the state. The history of the National Road is, arguably, the history of America itself, and Maryland's portion is loaded with palpable signposts. From the Colonial-era structures of old Baltimore to the nineteenth-century train depots scattered along the way; from the quirkily haunted frontier inns to the little mountain taverns where George Washington stopped; from the blood-soaked ground of Civil War battlefields to the time-capsule general stores and the encroaching urban sprawl of modern life—Maryland's old turnpike is the story of America spread across 192 miles of two-lane wonder.

I stop to stretch my legs along a sharp curve called Devil's Elbow, between Catonsville and Ellicott City, just outside of Baltimore along the old National Road.

"It's from all the motorists who die here," says Tony Poleski when I ask about the Devil's Elbow moniker. "Four people in the past two years—trying to make this nasty turn and dip." Poleski is a produce vendor along the Elbow, his sign saying: "You'll love our sweet corn." He talks more about the traffic: "We also have a problem with motorists hitting deer here."

I thank him for the information and get back in my car, driving the curve very slowly and with my eyes wide open. My snug seat belt suggests more than just the risks of modern car travel; it reminds me of the hundred-fold hazards faced by immigrant settlers with pack mules negotiating steep hills, swollen creeks, and hairpin curves with names like Devil's Elbow. Of course, 175 years ago the National Road running along this very curve was much cruder, only thirty feet wide and paved with rough stones. It was known to wash out and tear up bare feet and rattle the skulls of teamsters. But it was *the* superhighway of its time, and it fueled Baltimore's rise as a great port city with a surge of trade goods from the West, including barrels of Indian corn, bear grease, and furs from as far away as the Rockies.

Baltimore's still a big town, of course. I spend two hours getting in and out of downtown thanks to a trio of I-95 wrecks and an Orioles baseball game bottleneck. But now, with the Devil's Elbow behind me and deer in the vicinity, I'm finally feeling the freedom of the open two-lane road, my car pointed west.

A patchwork of contemporary road designations traces the National Road's original pioneer trail through Maryland—Scenic 40, Alternate 40, regular 40, and Maryland 144. It's the latter that takes me into the stone masonry of historic downtown Ellicott City, established 1772. On the edge of town, a two-hundred-year-old log cabin—with rope beds and candle lanterns—is preserved as a typical way station along the turnpike. At such places, located every ten miles or so, a teamster was sure to find an able blacksmith and a stable boy forking hay. Rates were standard: For $1.75 a teamster got his dinner, feed for six horses, and all the whiskey he could drink. Today, on summer weekends when he's not away on U.S. Navy duty, area resident Chris Petronis plays the role of an old turnpike road surveyor here, equipped with quill pen and old maps and a nineteenth-century range pole that keeps youngsters transfixed.

As I head west again on 144, the horrors of sprawl development threaten to poke holes in my time-travel trance. Cattle guards give way to gated subdivisions. Names like Oster Farm Road yield to Pink Dogwood Court. But eventually rural country prevails again, green and expansive, and the towns I pass through—Lisbon and New Market—are small, old, and "linear." These are old turnpike towns, with few cross streets and no downtown square because the businesses ran in a line along the pike, catering to travelers with road-facing taverns, inns, and stables. Many of these structures still remain, like New Market's old Utz Hotel (now Mealey's restaurant), where the original wooden pump for watering horses stands beside a fireplace that has warmed guests every year since 1836.

More than a few turnpike towns have smaller populations today than they did 150 years ago for the obvious reason that the road is utterly obsolete. Its demise, paradoxically, is also the story of America, as technological leaps in the form of canals, railroads, and finally, definitively, interstate highways, tapped the road's traffic. Today, the turnpike seems all but forgotten except by the small-town barbers, grocers, and farmers who live along its course. Nor has the road jelled as a tourist destination. Over the next three days, I won't meet a single traveler doing what I'm doing. Two of my three nights I'll be the only guest at old inns along the way.

All of which is immensely appealing. I feel, well, like a pioneer, pushing west on my own, blazing a trail that few people—alive, at least—have traveled in full. I'm thoroughly energized by this thought as I reach downtown Frederick and find a worn but dignified granite milepost marking the original turnpike outside Blueridge News and Spirits on East Patrick Street. A few blocks away, I admire a stretch called Shab Row—so named because it was once abandoned to a shabby, rundown appearance—where perfectly restored log structures once housed wheelwrights plying their trade for Conestoga teamsters.

For the gushing stream of wagons heading west, the suddenly mountainous landscape outside Frederick must have given pause. I follow Alternate 40 up and over a ridge called Braddock Heights just as the sun is setting. Passing Middletown, Maryland, whose small-town church-steeple charm is right out of New England, I begin the more serious climb up fabled South Mountain. This is just a warm-up for the bigger mountains west, but already I slip my car into low gear just before crossing the Appalachian Trail. I can't help but imagine the dusty, foot-sore drovers who once trudged up this slope with their bawling herd of cows or bleating sheep, sustained only by the promise of two-dollars-per-acre virgin land in the Ohio Valley still so very far away.

At the summit of South Mountain, at Turner's Gap, I arrive at arguably the most famous structure along the entire turnpike in Maryland: the Old South

Mountain Inn. Nearly 250 years old, it has served trail travelers continuously since 1790, first as an inn and—in more recent years—as a restaurant only. If ever one could will that stone walls speak, this would be the spot. Andrew Jackson took the National Road to his first inauguration—and stayed here. Abe Lincoln did the same as a freshman congressman in 1841. And George Washington almost certainly stopped here as a young Indian fighter.

But it's the inn's role in the Civil War that's on my mind as I order dinner with the day's last light seeping through beautiful diamond pane windows. For decades, the National Road was key to fueling America's westward expansion. That expansion, by 1861, threatened to tear North and South apart over the issue of slavery's spread west. After dinner, I visit the inn's imposing and somberly lighted Civil War Room, whose fifteen paintings commemorate the pivotal 1862 battle of South Mountain. In fighting all around this inn, Confederate general D.H. Hill held off a much larger Union force, thanks in part to a trick. Hill armed and sent to the front a band of cooks, teamsters, and camp aides, giving the impression of sizable reinforcements arriving from the turnpike. The trick worked, momentarily stalling a Union attack and saving the day—but not before four thousand men, Union and Confederate, had become casualties. A few minutes' walk from the inn, just off the turnpike, one hundred Confederates were buried by being stuffed down a drinking well.

You know you're a city boy out in the country when you plop down two dollars for a large coffee and morning newspaper, and the gas station attendant, embarrassed by your failing math skills, slides one dollar back to you even before operating the old cash register, which has raised buttons. *Cha-ching!*

This happens to me the next morning in tiny Funkstown, south of Hagerstown, where I begin to realize that Maryland is a different state on the other side of South Mountain. Here in the vast Cumberland Valley and beyond, where Irish workmen broke stones for the National Road in the 1820s, some of the surviving turnpike towns are so small that the only bar is the American

Legion post and the local paper's top story is not Kosovo but the nearby calf born with two mouths. Everything's just different on this side of the divide.

Forty miles farther down the road, in the microdot community of Wilson, west of Hagerstown, these differences deepen still. All I want is a soda as I enter the redbrick Wilson General Store, a historic resupplying spot for turnpike travelers for the past 149 years. I find no one inside, not even the proprietor. This gives me time to recover from the shock of stumbling into a world that would not have provoked a blink from my great-grandfather.

All around, nine-foot-tall oak shelves reach almost to the ceiling, laden with bolts of cloth, stick candy, and crude bricks of lye soap. A rear counter offers jarred whole pickles, dried hominy, and Frostburg bologna by the pound, regular or hot. A chalkboard on one wall announces, "Hay—$2.75 bale," and the whole place smells faintly of the stuff. Just behind the checkers table sits a potbelly stove glowing with locust oak logs and surrounded by a litter of eight-week-old kittens tumbling across the original plankwood floor.

Finally, a side door opens and thirty-eight-year-old store manager Mickey Stinger, boyishly handsome and in need of a shave, apologizes: "I didn't know you were here. I was selling feed next door."

Stinger quickly asserts that this is no tourist-bait diorama of nineteenth-century rural life. "It's a real, working general store," he says. "People drive forty miles for our cheddar cheese and farmers still buy their feed here." Still, he admits that the store's partly an informal history museum, with old wagon wheels and horse bridles from the trail days scattered about (and not for sale). The store seems to suffer from a general inability to throw things out. An 1853 ledger sheet on one wall shows that one of Stinger's ancestors owed the store twenty-seven cents. "But I'm not paying it back," Stinger chuckles. "No way. Can you imagine? With the interest?"

I buy my soda and, with some regret, prepare to leave, but not before Stinger offers me one of the store kittens on the way out. Of course, he also tells me to hurry back real soon. Amiable storekeepers like this—how many dozens over the years?—must account for the store's amazing survivability, I consider, including enduring the huge drop in turnpike traffic in the 1850s brought on by the C&O Canal and B&O Railroad.

Thirty minutes farther west down the turnpike in Hancock, I stop at the C&O Canal Visitors Center, operated by the National Park Service. Beginning in the late 1820s, the canal was hailed as "a dream passage to western wealth," with boats navigating sixty-one locks between Cumberland, Maryland, and Washington, D.C., taking coal and wheat downstream and finished goods upstream—just as turnpike wagons had once done. But by 1850, the greater speed and efficiency of railroads had done to the canal what the canal had done to the turnpike.

At any rate, by the 1880s, many turnpike settlements were nearly ghost towns—and some apparently are still haunted today. About four miles west of Hancock on Maryland 144, I find an old turnpike inn—now a private residence—in somewhat rundown condition beside a vast orchard of apple trees awash in sunset light. Mechanic Mark Neilson, sporting a hunting cap and grease-stained hands, tells me his family of six tries to keep the two-story inn's old boards and stone foundation in shape. But, I infer, there can't be much time left after caring for the family's Noah's Ark of yard animals, a spectacle that caused me to pull over in the first place. Neilson counts on his fingers: "One horse, three cows, one pig, one donkey, seven pheasants, ten geese, seven dogs, five cats, twelve chickens, twenty-six chicks, one turkey, two ducks, and four rabbits."

This happy, if crowded, home is also overrun by ghosts. Neilson's girlfriend has seen an apparition float through the bedroom at night, and everyone has heard chamber music fill the house, sans the aid of a single radio or stereo. Most amazing, a light in the dining room once came on by itself—*unplugged*. No one's quite sure what these "friendly" ghosts are trying to say, but it appears the walls of this old turnpike inn *are* trying to speak.

Still scarier than this is something that happens toward the end of my second day on the National Road: I'm forced to drive the interstate. Just past the town of Indian Springs and the old French and Indian War garrison of Fort

Relic Hunting on a Pioneer Trail

Frederick, the gentle and meandering two-lane 40 merges with four-lane I-70 for a six-mile stretch built right on top of the old turnpike. It's the first time since I left I-95 way back in Baltimore that my car has exceeded fifty mph. The sudden speed seems bizarre to me, fantastic, reckless, weird, a little dangerous. If I were in outer space, the stars would blur and streak from the effect of warp speed. This same blurring, of course, happens to all the small towns and landmarks along the adjoining landscape. Gone are the tilting, cast-iron historic markers and the hand-scrawled signs advertising apples by the bucket. It's all far away, incomprehensible, obliterated. I seem not to have left just the charisma of the old turnpike, but Earth itself. If American history is one of transportation changes that shape culture, then speed, interstate speed, is a transportation phenomenon whose attendant culture has no connection whatsoever to history or the land. We're going much too fast to comprehend either.

Not soon enough, the exit sign for Maryland 144 announces itself, taking me back to the old trail. I return to Earth.

Just west of Cumberland, in the town of LaVale, I find a seven-sided Toll Gate House with white-brick walls and a wood-shingled roof. It was built for the turnpike around 1833 and is well preserved today. Tolls were charged all along the National Road, with most of the money going to the young federal government for construction and maintenance of America's first federal highway. A sign quotes the tolls of 1833, including "6 cents for every hog" and "12 cents for every score of cattle."

I'm in the Maryland panhandle now, serious mountain country, in a county whose very name—Allegany—derives from the Native American word meaning "land of endless mountains." Farms become scarce along the turnpike, and thickly forested slopes lead to scenic lookouts where the mountains do indeed seem to roll west forever. I pass wild turkeys and deer along the road, and the entrances to state parks carry black bear warnings. Farther west still, steep climbs up Big Savage Mountain (2,900 feet) and Negro Mountain (3,075 feet) are part of the reason it took struggling wagoners about ten full days to travel the turnpike from Baltimore to the state's westernmost border. Today, Marylanders out here live in a world apart. They root for the Pittsburgh Pirates and Steelers, and you never see a Save the Bay license plate because the Chesapeake Bay might as well be part of the Eurasian steppe.

The economy in this region is generally depressed, though the people of Frostburg seem to have maintained a sense of humor. I pause along beautiful old Main Street at a coffee shop whose sign says Tombstone Cafe: A Unique Undertaking. It occupies an old, former shop for headstone sculptors. I sip my latte and try to imagine the warren of abandoned coal-mine tunnels running below the downtown streets of this fading old mining town.

More scenic mountain driving along Alternate 40 takes me to the glorious and very lonesome Casselman River Bridge, just east of Grantsville. This eighty-foot span of stone, built for the turnpike in 1813, includes a magnificently elongated arch engineered in anticipation of the canal traffic that never made it this far west.

It's just ten more miles to the Pennsylvania border and my journey's end. I stop, appropriately, at the State Line United Methodist Church. It's a frame one-room sanctuary built right on the border amid forested land abutting Pig's Ear Road. Seventy-year-old Ruth Wirthing, who lives across the street in Pennsylvania, sees me admiring the old country church.

"It's been here since the eighteen-hundreds," she says, gesturing toward the church's steeply pitched roof and old-fashioned arched windows. "It's been my church since the nineteen-thirties."

Wirthing walks over in her baseball cap and trousers and grows a bit nostalgic. Situated hard by the road, the church attracted turnpike travelers in the old days. Wirthing remembers as a child the Model Ts pulling over for Sunday service. This was a brief era of renaissance for the turnpike, when car travel was suddenly possible but the interstate system had not yet been invented. In those days, Wirthing's father had a lumber mill across the street, close enough to the turnpike for easy truck transport of boards to market.

Wirthing tells me she's part of a local historic society dedicated to preserving the heritage of the National Road. "This old turnpike," she says as we cross the narrow two lanes back toward her cedar-sided house, "has been part of our families here—part of who we are—for generations. We just don't want to forget what it's done for us or for this country."

I prepare to leave, fetching my car along Pig's Ear Road, when Wirthing adds, "You should come for church some time. You know how to find us now, right? Just follow the turnpike."

18

Night Train to Georgia with a Very Little Boy

So I'm traveling alone with my not quite three-year-old son on a night train to Georgia and everything starts out just fine. Charles, our sleeper-car attendant, dressed nattily in blue vest and tie, helps bring our heap of things on board: suitcases, stroller, sippy cup, storybooks, security blanket, bottle, lots of extra Spiderman underwear, and a toy locomotive that never leaves my son's hand.

"When's the train going to *go*?" Sasha asks me, his little-boy blue eyes now electric with anticipation. He smiles under the bill of an engineer's cap Charles has just given him.

"Soon," I say.

We're in downtown Washington, D.C., in historic Union Station on Amtrak track 25. Outside our car, passengers and luggage carts whiz by, postal workers toss sacks of letters onto mail cars, and safety engineers in hard hats check the four-thousand-horsepower diesel locomotives that will pull us 634 miles to Atlanta, arriving around nine-forty-five tomorrow morning.

"When's the train going to *go*?" Sasha asks again.

"Any minute," I say. "Let's go order dinner."

The dining car is two-and-a-half cars away, a trip made interminable by Sasha's insistence that *he* be the one to activate the sliding doors between cars with his silver-dollar size palms. We reach the diner, a place of elegant, old-fashioned charm with ten cushy booths, white tableclothes, soft lamplighting, and fresh carnations on each table.

"When I grow up, I'm going to be a *fast* locomotive!" Sasha tells the waitress bringing us menus.

"You *are*?" she says. "Well, we better feed you so you'll be strong too."

Then Sasha turns to me with a serious face and I know he's going to ask again about the train's departure. My son is a certified train fanatic, one who's been telling his friends for weeks he's taking a "sleeping train" to visit his grandparents. At home, we can practically build a skyscraper with all our train books and then connect the top floor to the moon with wooden Brio train track. Sasha's preschool teacher praises him as a laid-back kid with one exception: "He can get, well, a little aggressive over sharing trains," she says, clearing her throat.

My theory is that trains stir up ancient genetic memories in little boys, taking them back to the veldt where survival required an obsession—from birth—with mastodons and other big and noisy quarry. But genetic instincts die hard and slowly, which is why Big Things That Go still dominate our little boys' dreams in an ever-changing modern culture.

So I was happy to book a standard bunkbed compartment on Amtrak's Crescent line to Atlanta, giving my wife a five-day break from parenting in the process. More than just a boy's dream come true, train travel has a dramatically practical side: It's the only form of long-distance land travel that lets kids do their thing: roam, fidget, swing their elbows, have pillow fights. And certainly anyone who's tried to change a diaper at thirty thousand feet needs no further sales pitch.

Not that travel anywhere with a kid under three is all chocolates and leisure reading. For when Sasha turns to me that third time with a serious look on his face, it isn't to ask about the departure time.

"I need to make pee-pee!" he says.

I scoop him up and begin the mad dash. By standard reckoning I have about ninety seconds to get from the diner car to the toilet in our sleeper two-and-a-half cars away. But the diner is now full of aisle-blocking people and, beyond that, luggage litters the car hallways. At the end of one car, right in our way, is the train's chief of onboard services who's speaking into a microphone, addressing the entire train. That's why passengers from all across the eastern seaboard hear a crazed father's background voice: "Excuse me! Excuse me! My son's gotta go! My son's gotta *go!*"

I quickly realize we'll never make it. I spot a hallway door marked Shower and dash in. There's no toilet, just a drain on the floor. Sasha bursts into tears as I yank down his britches: "I wanna toilet! I wanna toilet!" he says. He goes anyway, his copious tears joining the flow down to the drain as his refrain changes to "I want my mommy."

And that's when it happens. The train jerks and lurches and begins rolling. Our grand, long-anticipated departure finally comes while we're in midstream, inside a cramped shower, having a certified meltdown. We waited weeks and weeks for *this?* I wonder.

But I soon discover something: The ultimate tonic for meltdown hysteria is the *clickity-clack* of rails and the sight of the whole world passing before your dining car window. "There's Bill Clinton's house!" Sasha squeals with adorable inaccuracy, all smiles now, as the floodlit Capitol building gets smaller and smaller in the distance and we chug across the Potomac River. All around us dishes clink, and people chatter just like at a real restaurant, and a cook with a tall chef's hat prepares Maryland old bay crab cakes in the back kitchen. For Sasha, whose cheeks are still moist from tears, I order a kid's plate called The Little Fireman. Then I turn to the waitress:

"One very, very cold beer please."

The locomotive sends a lonely horn blast into the dark countryside of central Virginia and the cars rock rhythmically from side to side as Sasha and I make our way back to our sleeper compartment, hand in hand, our bodies swaying. During dinner, Charles has taken the liberty of neatly preparing our bunkbeds, turning down the covers to form perfect triangles. Then, as if to trump the amazing presence of Ghirardelli mint chocolates on our pillows, he turns to me with his handsome mustache and faint southern drawl and asks, "Can I bring you coffee and a newspaper with your wake-up call in the morning?"

Who says proud and professional train service went the way of the dodo decades ago?

"By all means," I tell Charles. It's comforting to know that while I take complete care of Sasha on this long journey, someone else is taking very good care of me.

Inside our compartment, Sasha and I test the narrow but comfortable mattresses and delight in having two fluffy pillows each. We face the inescapable fact: Our compartment may be very small, even evoking the feel of a cocoon, but at least it's big enough for a pillow fight. And that's how the uniformed chief of services, Richard, finds us: pillows flying everywhere, one landing in the hallway. Richard's the same guy I nearly ran over earlier during the pee-pee crisis. I apologize for that incident.

"Don't worry about it," he says, kindly handing Sasha a small teddy bear dressed in engineer's overalls and cap, courtesy of the Crescent crew. "When you've traveled as much as me, you've seen it all. I've traveled four million miles in my life." Then, so as not to appear boastful, he says, "Of course, two-

and-a-half million of those miles were for work." (Note: Four million miles equals about eight round-trips to the moon.)

Richard leaves and we close our door and draw the door shade and now it's just Sasha and me in our tiny room. Two horizontal bands of long, wonderful windows parallel our bunks, letting in the dim light of passing farmhouses and the flashing, dinging red of crossing guards and the late-night street lamps of towns too small to warrant station stops. The whole outer wall of this compartment really is just one big window, and Amtrak's name for this sleeper car—*The Viewliner*—seems especially apt as a panorama of stars comes into view above the ever-darkening rural landscape.

The *Viewliner* cars were designed and brought into service by Amtrak in 1996, and they still have a freshly minted look. The cars replaced the old *Heritage* sleepers built in the late 1940s and famous for their broken doors and toilets that didn't work in their later years. But looking around our compartment now I'm pressed to name an additional comfort that could have reasonably been included. There's a music system, hideaway washbasin, ice water dispenser, large mirror, commode, even an individual climate control unit.

And of course there's a color video monitor for watching movies. It's happened on buses, planes, even minivans, so why not trains, right? Perhaps we'll soon be able to eliminate the hassles of travel altogether by hiring stand-in cameramen to take our trips for us, sending back edited videos.

Our family's not real big on TV, but I'll admit it was handy having something to freeze Sasha in place for ten minutes—a Disney Tarzan film did it— while I got his pajamas down from a storage compartment and prepared a soy-milk bedtime bottle. Remarkably, despite being on a train speeding at up to seventy-nine miles an hour through the Virginia piedmont, our bedtime ritual is virtually unchanged from what we'd do at home. We both lie on Sasha's bed (the lower bunk) and read three books together. Then he drinks his bottle. Then I tell him a story (a train and a baby whale have a race). Then he squeezes his security blanket and gives me a kiss and we lie side by side until he falls asleep.

The compartment lights are all off now, and the gentle rocking and swaying of the train seems even more conspicuous and comforting in the dark. Uncharacteristically, Sasha stirs very little before drifting off—and no wonder. If automobiles are famous for knocking out even the most colicky of babies, imagine what the pronounced *clickity-clack* of a train will do.

We listen in the dark to that sound: the train's heavy wheels rolling over steel bars set atop a seemingly infinite blur of wooden ties. Then comes the blow of the train's horn, over and over again, low and guttural like a big bass harmonica, as we weave past little Virginia towns with names like Dry Fork and Sweet Briar and Woodberry Forest. I imagine the lead locomotive's headlights up ahead knifing through the blackness just as another horn blast comes—a long groan followed by a short blast—drowning out the clack of the rails, then the clack comes back.

I'm suddenly amazed at what an antique arrangement this is, virtually unchanged since the dawn of rail travel. Sasha insists that we're sleeping in the train's coal car. The locomotive is up front of us so we must be in the coal car, just behind. And while coal isn't what's fueling this train in the year 2000, these sounds filling our ears harken back to that long-ago era and beyond. Someone traveling by sleeper in 1950 or 1900 or 1850 would not blink an eye if transported to the dark of our sleeper car in 2000, hearing what we're hearing, feeling the rock of these rails.

In a disposable society where a car is considered old after three years and baseball stadiums are blown up after thirty and half of all marriages don't last, it's good to know that at least one thing endures. My two-and-a-half-year-old son is traveling by sleeper car, hearing these sounds, rocked to sleep by a train, in the twenty-first century.

There's a sudden movement next to me in the bed.

"Daddy?" Sasha whispers.

"Yes?" I say.

There's no immediate response, then he puts his mouth gently to my ear and, in the faintest possible whisper, says, "We're sleeping with the train, Daddy."

It's the last thing he says, then he's gone for good and I'm left wondering for the millionth time how my heart still fits in my chest with all the love it holds for this little boy.

At 7:00 A.M. Charles knocks on the door and, true to his word, he has coffee and a copy of the Sunday Greenville (S.C.) *News*. Sasha is still fast asleep, clutching his engineer teddy bear, so I luxuriate with coffee and sports scores in bed, warm and dry despite the heavy spring rain driving against my window and soaking the state of South Carolina passing by outside.

Down here, in early April, the dogwoods and redbuds are in full bloom, two weeks ahead of D.C. I see fields of shocking red clay and whole hillsides of kudzu vines. The train clearly covered lots of ground while Sasha and I slept.

I hear a stirring below me and then Sasha starts whimpering. He's a famously grumpy waker-upper, and he's confused by his surroundings. "I want my mommy," he says, starting to cry. I say nothing as I hop down to his bunk. The night before I had drawn closed the pleated curtains across his window to keep out any light. Now, with Sasha's eyes filling with tears and my ears filling with his cries, I simply open those curtains—*sssffftttt!*—and he's instantly silent. Like magic, a wooden stable full of horses zooms by. Then a patch of thick, enchanted forest. Then pickup trucks carrying bales of hay on a gravel road. While Sasha meditates on this great pageant of sights, still in bed, still in his PJs, I get his clothes, socks, shoes, and toothbrush ready to start the day. Who needs TV after all?

We suddenly go through a short, dark tunnel. "This is a strawberry cat food tunnel!" Sasha says. It makes no sense at all. He laughs out loud. His mood couldn't be better.

The dining car is busy by the time we arrive for breakfast. A waitress taking someone's order yells back to the kitchen, "Fran, you got any more oatmeal?"

207

Hungry and well rested, we order pancakes and scrambled eggs, then feel sorry for the people back in coach wandering in with rumpled clothes, massaging their necks. We share a booth with Bill and Becky, a middle-aged couple from Atlanta traveling home by sleeper from a Boston business meeting. The journey is twenty-four hours long.

"Why not just fly?" I ask them as the train conductor passes through, checking tickets. The conductor winks at Sasha and calls him "partner."

"Why not fly?" says Bill. "Because you're cattle on airplanes these days. They pack you in and could care less about your comfort. The seat space gets smaller every year. You have communal toilets, lousy food, plastic forks, and flight attendants who'd rather be digging ditches.

"But this," he says, motioning to his link sausages and omelet garnished with an orange slice, his shiny silverware and cloth napkin and the fresh carnations by the window that seem to frame the countryside passing by outside, "*This* is more civilized."

"More coffee?" the waitress asks, stopping by to top off all our cups.

Bill continues, "In terms of money and time, yes it's a bit of a splurge to travel by train sleeper. But what good is life if you can't enjoy the journey from point A to B?"

By the time Sasha and I return to our compartment, Charles has pressed the upper bunk to the ceiling and converted the lower into two well-cushioned, face-to-face chairs. We read books, have another pillow fight, then pretend we're bad dinosaurs who sneeze and blow down the houses passing by outside.

The train rolls into Gainesville, Georgia, the last stop before Atlanta. Richard, the head attendant, announces over the PA that there's a seventy-one-year-old man detraining here to begin hiking the nearby Appalachian Trail all the way to Maine.

"He's walking all the way back to Onion Station?" Sasha asks. He means D.C.'s Union Station.

"Even farther," I say.

Night Train to Georgia with a Very Little Boy

Finally, just slightly behind schedule, we arrive in Atlanta and I carry Sasha off while Charles deposits our luggage on the platform and congratulates Sasha for being such a good train traveler. Sasha and I each have serious bed head, but otherwise we're in good shape, well fed and alert. Last night in D.C. we stepped into a rolling bedroom. Then we ate, slept, and ate again. Then we stepped out of that bedroom. Who could be saddle sore?

Up ahead we see Sasha's grandfather, aunt, uncle, and three cousins, all come to welcome us. Sasha is shy at first, but then snaps out of it as the locomotives begin pulling away for the long haul on down to New Orleans.

"We slept on the train!" Sasha tells his cousins. "We slept on the train!"

VI
Departure

19

Small Paradise in the Congo

The oldest man in this clan of African Pygmies pulls out a sharp knife from his grass belt and begins walking directly toward Karen, my girlfriend, who's stiffening by my side. We're surrounded by no fewer than ten half-naked Pygmy men, none much taller than four-and-a-half feet, all armed with machetes, spears, knives, and nets. One of these men has killed an elephant single-handedly, using only a spear in this rain forest deep inside the Congo.

The Pygmy elder draws closer and closer to Karen, his knife blade now heading directly for her neck. She stands perfectly still. Most of the men around us are whooping and yelling excitedly. Some have begun making violent gunshot noises by slapping their hands against their chests in a strange way. The younger men have been smoking marijuana from long pipes made from the branches of banana trees. Wild-eyed, they now work themselves into a frenzy, shouting at us, shouting at the surrounding forest, shouting at each other.

We certainly never expected this when we hired a machete-wielding guide for the half-day trek through dense forest to this prehistoric camp of crude stick shelters and spear-toting people. Lost in an ocean of teakwood and mahogany trees soaring as high as two hundred feet overhead, these Pygmy people, called the Mbuti, are perhaps the most tradition-bound human beings on Earth. They hunt wild animals on foot and without guns, gathering mushrooms and berries and other fruit along the way. They lack fire-starting technology, carrying with them smoldering embers wrapped in leaves each time they break camp and move on in their interminable nomadic wandering through the boundless forest.

Just getting to this remote spot has been extremely difficult for Karen and me. For days we traveled across the breadth of the Democratic Republic of the Congo, that vast, sprawling, untamed nation stretching like a mighty hand across most of Central Africa. After a short plane ride up from the mouth of the Congo River, we boarded a falling-down riverboat and for seven days chugged upstream to the town of Kisangani, the navigable end of the Congo's mighty flow and the location of Joseph Conrad's harrowing, fictitious "final station" in the novel *Heart of Darkness*. From here we boarded a series of wheezing transport trucks and continued east, sitting atop bags of rice and beside bleating goats for thirty hours over barbarously rutted dirt roads. We hopped down with our backpacks only after reaching the Epulu River, the heart of the legendary Ituri Forest, that far-flung middle section of a rain forest band stretching fantastically from Uganda to the Atlantic Ocean. We are now at the precise geographic center of the continent, what Henry Morton Stanley called "Darkest Africa," a rain forest so lush and thick that only scattered beams of sunlight break a dusky interior filled with endless lianas and creepers and the chatter of black-and-white Colobus monkeys.

Small Paradise in the Congo

This is the setting for the Mbuti Pygmy knife incident. The clan had seemed pleased enough with our gifts of sardines and salt as we ambled into their camp, wet to our thighs from crossing several streams during the ten-mile jungle hike in. This is a green, cool, shady world full of colorful large leaves and flowering trees, where the tracks of wild pigs and dik-dik antelope dot the trails and the calls of invisible birds float down from the treetops. The pupils of our eyes, when we arrive, are nearly the size of dimes from the impossible daytime darkness of the forest.

For hours the situation is quite friendly. Then the Pygmies announce it is time to go hunting and we all stand. That's when the clan elder faces Karen—a fit, fair-skinned twenty-four-year-old—and takes out his knife and guides it closer and closer to her neck. Then he starts cutting. Karen doesn't flinch at all, primarily because this gentle chief, who never stops smiling the whole time and wouldn't hurt a fly, holds her hair in such a way that it doesn't hurt as he slices through twenty or so strands. That's all he wants: a lock of her hair.

And when he finishes cutting the hair and holds up the lock for the rest of the clan to see, all the Mbuti men and women and children in camp start laughing uproariously as if they've just heard the funniest joke in the world. Still smiling and laughing, they pat us on our backs good-naturedly as if to congratulate us.

"With this hair," says the elder in the local Kingwana tongue, "we will surely have a successful hunt."

He then ties the lock to the top of a hunting net designed especially for catching antelope and forest buffalo. Years before, the clan had caught lots of animals using "European" hair as a good luck charm—and now it's time to try again.

So we all plunge into the forest, single file, with the Pygmies still laughing and hooting and hollering about the hair-cutting matter. They are a charmingly excitable people who seem to make up for their small stature by making loud and continuous noises. Everyone is extra happy to be off on the afternoon hunt, hungry for the forest's daily offering. Some of the Pygmies break into song and others stop for a quick, spontaneous dance as we edge farther and farther into the dark sea of trees to catch wild animals.

These memories of hunting with Mbuti Pygmies float back to me across the span of thirteen years as I sit at my writing table beside a wide-open office window. It is January 3, 2000, a point in time overwrought with zeroes and, for me, worries about the future. Outside, in the outskirts of Washington, D.C., the temperature on this mid-winter day is an appalling 66 degrees Fahrenheit. I am at north latitude 39 degrees and west longitude 77 degrees, where the "normal" low temperature for this time of year in this part of North America is in the hard-freezing mid-twenties. Instead, forsythia bushes across the street in my neighbor's yard are blooming with delicate yellow petals under a shirtsleeve-warm sun.

The weather is too disturbing, too abnormal, to enjoy. It distracts me for a moment from writing anything more about the Pygmies. Perhaps what's happening outside my window *isn't* global warming. Perhaps it's just a fluke. But it's certainly getting harder and harder to close our eyes and hum nursery rhymes to drown out the incoming data. I check the next day's newspaper and find that yesterday's 66 degrees was a record high for the date. Tellingly, the record that was *broken* was not from January 1891 or 1933, not some long-ago freak heat wave that only our grandparents remember. No, the previous record for January third in Washington was set in 1997, just thirty-six months back. And the record before that was set in 1991. When days of never-before-seen warm weather form a record-book traffic jam just a few years apart, spilling into the new century, isn't that what's commonly known as a trend?

I have a Canadian friend, Neil, a journalist, who spent last summer reporting on the changing lives of Inuit people inside the Arctic Circle. Neil says these people are now seeing mosquitoes across their landscapes in swarms they've never witnessed before. More disturbing, their centuries-old oral history makes no reference to so many mosquitoes or to the newly arriving varieties of beetles and sand flies. For the Inuit, climate change is no half-baked theory or left-wing conspiracy—not as they watch, horrified, as caribou drown by the thousands each year atop previously reliable ice bridges that are melting away completely, ending an animal migration that has sustained the Inuit since time immemorial.

Climate change is more pronounced at the poles, of course, where, for example, it rained briefly at the American base on Antarctica's McMurdo Sound during the southern summer of 1997. Meteorologists, stumped for a way to convey just how freaky liquid precipitation is at this bastion of extreme cold, say it is the weather-oddity equivalent of a snowstorm in Saudi Arabia.

But why worry about climate upheaval and chaos in the new century when we've developed such excellent coping skills? Type the words "magic wand" in your newly interactive on-line dictionary and you're likely to get a very short definition: silicon chip. Never mind the two-hundred-billion-dollar stupidity of double-digit date fields employed right up to the millennial rollover. We're technologically immune. Immortal. What could go wrong when soon we'll have genetically engineered pigs with four hind legs to conveniently double our ham? Or self-fertilizing, non-pollinating, poison-laced petro-corn? We'll have Frankenfood on every plate across the vast globalized dinner table, all of it guaranteed safe, USDA signed and sealed.

Of course, like the Pygmies on their hunt, we'll surely need some luck charm to see us through. *Forever* just isn't a word that attaches itself well to a culture built on cars and machines that completely remake the third planet from the sun, changing its core characteristics, cooking its air. And DNA surgery on living things, the long-range consequences of which no one can foretell, does not inspire visions of equilibrium and sustainability, of meeting societal needs without jeopardizing the ability of future generations to meet their own needs. Balance just isn't part of this deal now on offer.

So I don't think it makes me a Luddite to say I see nothing perfectible about a society flinging itself in this particular direction. Indeed, as I look back on twenty years of travel across six continents, and as I ponder what I've learned, I realize something very important: I've already seen the perfect society. I've witnessed the best that humans can be. It's not a vision that came to

217

me via the hallucinogenic brew of an Andean medicine man. Neither is it an intellectual ideal I've soberly cobbled together, taking the best of different cultures I've seen to make a fanciful mental composite. And it certainly has nothing whatsoever to do with our western steamroller culture barreling toward an ecologically crippled future lined with plastic.

No, I've actually *been* to this perfect place. I've met these perfect people. I've seen the lavish wealth, the ridiculously short workdays, the tight-knit and caring families, the utterly sustainable economy based on ecological respect.

So if I could have just one wish fulfilled for our species and our future, it would be this: Let us all be transported, forever, magically, to the Ituri Forest.

Let us all be Mbuti Pygmies.

Up ahead, through the dense tangle of vines and jungle undergrowth, I make out a slight clearing. I shift the weight of my backpack to one side and stretch my neck to see a little better. I gaze right over the head of our Mbuti guide, Moko, who weighs only one hundred pounds and carries a huge hunting net over his shoulders like a cape.

"This is it," says Moko, gesturing with his machete. "The place where we live."

After hiking all morning and greatly anticipating this moment, it is still a shock to see, right before us, a scene from 10,000 B.C. Below a dim haze of sunlight filtering lazily through the treetops stands a tight circle of ten conical shelters, each looking like a small, leafy igloo barely five feet high. The huts are made of a framework of bent tree saplings covered entirely with large heart-shaped leaves in the fashion of shingles.

Inside the shelters there are no beds or mats or even blankets—just mounds of soft leaves atop which the Mbuti sleep each night. These crude shelters are grouped around a smoldering community fire sending up wisps of languid smoke toward the screech of unseen birds in faraway branches. Around the fire, on fallen tree trunks, a half-dozen Mbuti men sit. A few smoke tobacco from bamboo pipes. One man mends a net with a special forest vine. Another sharpens a wide-bladed spear against a stone.

Small Paradise in the Congo

Farther back from the fire, a shirtless woman nurses a baby asleep across her chest in a cloth sling, and a teenage girl enters the camp carrying a large gourd full of water from a nearby stream. Altogether there are about twenty men, women, and children in this camp, living in a virtual state of nature save for the frayed secondhand Western trousers on the men and the colorful wraparound cloth skirts in the African style on the women.

But what I remember most about that first glimpse into the Mbuti world is the laughter. Huge howls of mirth emanate from every quarter of the camp, rising from every clan member. The Pygmies, in fact, barely seem to notice as we pull into camp, so totally pinned are they to some side-splitting story—unintelligible to us—being told by a man around the fire. Two younger men are laughing with such abandon that they have to hold onto each other for support. Other men and women slap their sides and snap their fingers and go through all manner of physical contortions. One man is literally rolling on the ground, weeping with laughter. I've never seen people in such a state.

Reflexively, Karen and I smile and chuckle ourselves, instantly amused by the sheer, contagious joy of these stone-age comics.

Finally, the clan elder, a man in his sixties named Ageronga, notices we've arrived and walks over to greet us, wiping tears from his eyes while the hooting continues behind him. (We later learn the story is about an Mbuti child who fell harmlessly off a log bridge because he got a butterfly caught in his hair.)

I had read that the Mbuti Pygmy culture, despite a rapidly modernizing outside world, had changed little in thousands of years. Firsthand evidence of this comes almost immediately when Ageronga does something very odd after meeting us.

We'd brought with us an interpreter, a non-Pygmy African named Malamba, a member of the tribe of taller BaBira people who farm on the forest's edge. We speak French with Malamba, who speaks Kingwana with the Pygmies.

Ageronga politely shakes our hands and asks how our hike was into the forest. As we speak, he pulls out a small knife and begins casually—and curiously—cutting four thin, straight branches from a small tree edging the thick forest wall just a few feet away. Each branch is about three feet long. Ageronga listens attentively and nods in a friendly way as we explain that we are travelers from America with a special interest in traditional cultures. All the while, he's still fidgeting with those sticks. Soon he starts cutting a thin strip of vine from a certain forest bush an arm's-length away. He twists and ties the vine around the middle of the bundle of sticks. Then, in an act that seems like magic, he stands the bundle upon the ground right in front of us and, with a turn of his hand, splays out the ends until the sticks are slanting and intersecting in a freestanding structure like the metal legs of a backyard barbecue grill.

It's a chair.

"Please sit down," he says to Karen.

In just three or four minutes, using only forest materials within arm's reach, Ageronga has made a chair. Amazed, Karen sits down and declares the chair quite comfortable. A few ridiculously short minutes later, Ageronga has finished a chair for me.

Over the next two days we will watch this phenomenon again and again. Need a plate for your food? Just reach for a heart-shaped *mungango* leaf from that tree right behind you. Need a cup for drinking? Pick up an empty gourd by the fire. Need a basket for carrying forest game? Cut a few vines, tie a few knots, and voila: an on-the-spot tool. Instant wealth. Even the Mbuti huts— their very *houses*—take no more than an hour to build.

The resources of the forest are so abundant, and the Mbuti lifestyle so ingenious, that the clan lives almost entirely on what's simply laying around. They have no need for domestic animals and do not plant crops of any kind, opting for a hunter-gatherer way of life that some anthropologists have described as the oldest and most successful adaptation that man has ever made to his environment. With just a few simple tools, techniques, and weapons, the roughly forty thousand widely scattered Mbuti people make a living that keeps them physically healthier and living longer than any people I've seen across Africa. It also makes them seemingly happier than any people I've visited anywhere in the world.

Small Paradise in the Congo

Karen and I rest in our instamatic Mbuti chairs, glad to be off our feet after the long trek in. We have no idea where we are in this tropical rain forest, having been totally disoriented by the meandering trails that led us here.

Earlier that morning, we had met Moko and his family by the edge of the two-lane dirt road that serves as the only major east-west "highway" through the fifty-thousand-square-mile Ituri Forest. Almost immediately upon entering the forest in a single-file line behind Moko, who serves as our guide, we realize we are putting our lives completely into his hands. So lush and impossibly dense is the jungle undergrowth that just one hundred paces into it we are hard-pressed to guess which way leads back to the road. For most of the journey, visibility is only ten yards and I cannot discern the existence of any trail at all.

Yet Moko never hesitates, taking us on a twisting, turning route with great confidence while Karen and I lose all sense of direction. We stomp and stumble along awkwardly, trying to keep up, while the Mbuti seem to make no noise at all with their small feet, stepping so lightly they more or less float over the soft, leafy forest floor.

Contrary to the gloomy, evil feeling predicted by a century of colonial myth-making, this shady rain forest has a cheerful, welcoming atmosphere. We pass giant flowering trees and inhale the rich fragrance of red orchids shyly hiding their heads behind moss-covered upper branches. Here too live a plethora of brightly colored birds, including the rare Congo peacock, which meanders along sparkling-clear rivers and through a bewildering wealth of plant life so varied that up to fifty different species of trees exist in a single acre.

Furthering this bright atmosphere are the joyful voices of the Mbuti themselves. Throughout the hike, Moko, his wife, and their ten-year-old son talk and laugh boisterously and call out to one another. The loud banter forms a wonderful cascade of sound that echoes back and forth through the depths of the forest. The family happily discusses the bartering they did with the BaBira farming people along the road, exchanging fresh antelope meat for the few things the forest can't provide: metal pots, tobacco, a few plantains. Moko's wife carries a small piece of smoldering wood from the family's temporary roadside camp. Like most Mbuti, she eschews western matches for this more self-sufficient, millenia-old system.

The almost nonstop talk and loud laughter among the Mbuti has more than a social function. There are few dangers in the forest, but wild buffalo and leopards will attack without warning if startled suddenly—so Moko and family keep up the racket. Less threatening mammals in this virgin jungle include gorillas, chimpanzees, okapis, elephants, monkeys, dwarf hippos, and tree hyraxes.

We push through a final stretch of jungle undergrowth full of intertwined lianas, bushes, saplings, and reeds, and there it is: the camp. Karen and I rest in our homemade chairs while Moko and family unload their charges. Moko then sits by the community fire and smokes tobacco from a gourd pipe while his wife begins making twine from a vine called *nkusa* to repair the family's homemade hunting net, which will soon be used to great effect.

Moko eventually spawns a whole new round of camp laughter with stories about the supposedly hapless BaBira people with whom he has just traded. The Mbuti regularly make fun of the taller, agricultural BaBira, judging them incomprehensibly strange for their habit of living along roads and cutting down the forest instead of living off the forest's boundless riches. As migrants to the region, the BaBira don't fully understand the forest and its ways. Instead, they farm along its periphery, engaging in a backbreaking work vulnerable to drought and plague. These hardships lead them to view their world as rife with evil, where bad spirits capriciously make mischief in their lives. They likewise view the dense forest as a strange, forbidding, menacing place full of danger and malevolent forces. So the BaBira rarely venture far into the forest for any reason, relying on the Mbuti to provide them with fresh forest meat via trade.

For the Mbuti, nothing could be more different. There is little hardship in their world. They pretty much have all they want all the time, so there is no need to believe in bad spirits. To them, the forest is good, the world is good, their god is good, life is good.

And it's about to get better.

Late afternoon arrives, bringing with it scattered beams of golden sunlight that stream down to the forest floor. The conversations around the camp grow more animated with each passing minute. There's an excitement building. A shirtless man seated by the fire stands and places one hand over his heart as if to say a pledge. The bent arm is pressed against his chest in such a way that it creates a triangular cavity framed by his elbow, armpit, and wrist. Over this cavity the man suddenly brings down the opened palm of his other hand like a sledgehammer. The effect is like that of a powerful gun going off, piercing our ears and echoing loudly through the forest. Karen and I nearly fall from our seats, startled, while the Mbuti erupt in whoops of laughter and shouts of approval.

Two more men stand to make the gunshot noises while another begins screaming at the surrounding forest at the top of his lungs: "*Ngama'e! Ngama'e! Ngama'e!* There's an animal out there!"

It's time to go hunting.

A spirited debate ensues over which direction the hunting party should go. Half the clan wants to go east, the other north. There's a fair amount of bickering and frustrated yelling among these people who seem incapable of restraining their emotions no matter what the circumstances. I'm impressed to see the Mbuti women participate fully in the discussion. Indeed, an older woman with a crooked smile finally carries the day, passionately persuading the others to go north in the end.

Within the Mbuti's remarkably democratic system of self-government, women are accepted as pretty much equal to men. Group decisions are made with their full participation, and everyone's opinion is given equal consideration. Such customs are highly unusual in the rest of Africa, not to mention the rest of the world.

With the direction decided, the men begin preparing for the hunt. They place their tightly coiled hunting nets upon their shoulders and sharpen their knives and spears against a stone.

Three of the men pull out a five-foot-long banana tree branch. The green, slightly arching branch has a hollow interior that serves perfectly as a pipe. At the fat end the men attach a bowl made from a special forest leaf twisted into the shape of a cone. The men fill this bowl with copious amounts of marijuana and proceed to get thoroughly stoned, placing the narrow end of the branch to their mouths. Each time they draw on the pipe, which is longer than the men are tall and looks like some sort of long medieval trumpet, the men exhale great clouds of reefer smoke that literally cause their head and shoulders to disappear.

Now all the members of the clan are on their feet and getting ready—men, women, elders, young children—everyone. The camp is positively abuzz with chatter. There are more bizarre gunshot noises, and more people begin yelling out to the forest animals they now intend to capture: *"Ngama'e! Ngama'e!"*

A young man gathers embers from the community fire and starts a smaller fire at the base of a large tree at the edge of the camp. He throws on twigs and lots of leaves, creating dense clouds of smoke that billow up to the invisible sky. This is a sacred fire, one all Mbuti people light before a hunt to wake up the forest. Karen and I watch as Moko, Nkongongo, and all the others gather around the smokey fire for a moment of silence. There is no great ritual or ceremony, just this quiet standing around. But this act puts the hunters in harmony with the forest and secures its blessing and assistance for the day's hunt.

Moko later explains to me that the Mbuti believe in an all-powerful god who created the great forest and everything in it, including the Mbuti. The forest people logically reason that their god is good and loving because he provides the Mbuti with so many riches, satisfying all their needs. When bad things occasionally happen like an illness or an unsuccessful hunt, the Mbuti can only conclude that their benevolent god has fallen asleep. He's not aware that his "children" are unwell or hungry. So the smokey ceremonial fire prior to each hunt wakes up the forest and draws the attention of the Mbuti god, ensuring a successful outing.

Of course, it doesn't hurt to have a good-luck charm too, which is why Ageronga cuts off a lock of Karen's straight brown hair and ties it to a section of his net.

Small Paradise in the Congo

Everything is now set and our party proceeds into the forest in a single-file line, with Karen and me towering over our much shorter companions. As before, the forest immediately envelops us, smothering us with dense green vegetation, and I lose all sense of direction. Karen and I are near the middle of this line of twenty or so people, yet we can see only five people ahead of us before the human chain disappears completely. Overhead, in a maze of vines, handsome Colobus monkeys leap from perch to perch, watching us with great curiosity.

Each Mbuti woman carries a large woven basket, and now and then a woman leaves the line, disappearing through the forest's leafy curtain. Moments later she hurries back carrying a handful of edible mushrooms or forest fruit. Year-round, on forest walks like this, the women gather rich offerings, collecting all manner of roots, nuts, snails, grubs, termites, ants, larvae, and occasionally freshwater crabs and fish to supplement the catch of wild game from the hunt.

Five minutes into the hunting expedition I realize something. The Mbuti have grown silent. For the first time that day, they are making no noise whatsoever. The reason is obvious: We're on a quest for skittish forest animals. But the effect is startling nonetheless after the day-long profusion of human laughter, yelling, howling, talking, and chest slapping.

Soon this stealthy silence pays off. From the front of the line, hand signals are passed back indicating an antelope is somewhere to our right. The line comes to a halt. Karen and I are instructed to stay right where we are while an amazing orchestra of cooperative effort unfolds around us. The eight men carrying nets fan out in either direction through the trees, creating a giant semicircle with roughly two hundred feet between each hunter. The men uncoil their nets one after the other as they go, making a continuous chain. The nets are each about four feet wide and at least two hundred feet long, and the men hang them vertically all along the semicircle by attaching the woven mesh to the ubiquitous, ready-made support of tree branches and forest shrubs. This creates a formidable and highly camouflaged fence of netting.

Departure

Meanwhile, the Mbuti women and children quietly walk along one side of the semicircle until they reach the wide mouth of this U-shaped wall of nets. They station themselves in this opening, waiting for a signal telling them the nets are all well secured. Then the hunt begins. The women and children start clapping their hands and banging sticks together and screaming ferociously in high-pitched voices. They keep up the noise as they walk slowly toward the nets, entering the semicircle. In theory, any animal who happens to have been encircled by this quickly established perimeter of nets and people will flee the noise in the direction of the nets, where it will quickly get entangled.

Of course, Karen and I can see none of this happening. We've been instructed to stand and monitor a section of netting near the center of the giant crescent. On either side of us, just ten yards away, the mesh wall disappears completely into greenery. As for the loud-shouting women and children perhaps seventy-five yards in front of us, we can only hear them, not see them, as they get closer.

Within seconds the net we're monitoring begins jerking and bouncing. Somewhere to our left, beyond sight, an animal has become caught. We leave our post and follow the suddenly whooping voices of several Mbuti men to the scene of capture. A large bushbuck antelope, weighing perhaps 150 pounds, is hopelessly entangled. It struggles mightily, its small, sharp horns slashing dangerously. In a flash, three Mbuti hunters are on top of it. Two hold it down while a third cuts its throat with a knife.

We have been gone from camp perhaps twenty minutes and already we have more than a day's worth of meat for the entire clan. After just twenty *minutes.*

The Mbuti men immediately begin slaughtering the bushbuck while the arriving women and children start cutting special vines and quickly weave— on the spot—two crude backpacks with which to carry the quarry. Everyone is talking at the same time and yelling and laughing about this fine catch, their Pygmy love for boisterousness returning immediately, infused with great joy. Moments later, two women are chosen to carry the meat back to camp while the rest of us gather up the nets and strike off again into the forest for a second round of hunting.

Within an hour, using the same method, we've caught two more smaller bushbucks and the outlandishly successful hunt is called off. By the time we return to camp in the gathering darkness we've been gone less than two hours. All the fresh meat is piled atop a series of stick tables constructed right then. Small mounds of mushrooms and various fruit, gathered along the way, lie inside the leafy huts. It's an embarrassment of riches, born of the two-hour workday.

Ageronga, the oldest member of the clan, begins actively overseeing the division of the meat among the several families, settling a couple of brief disputes between neighbors in the process. Ageronga is not a chief. He has no formal authority or power, nor does anyone else in the clan. Headmen simply don't exist among the Mbuti. The status of an individual male depends mainly on his reputation as a hunter; a woman's on her gathering skills. An older man like Ageronga who is highly regarded as a hunter and has a reputation for modesty and wisdom will have some influence in camp affairs, but even he cannot acquire formal authority because it simply is not an aspect of life the Mbuti recognize.

The social imperative to cooperate in all things (no one, after all, can hunt with a net alone) ensures a level of mutual respect and consideration that preserves harmony. There is no official government within Mbuti society. No council. No army. No police. Just an emphasis on cooperative effort combined with a respect for individual liberty. Chronic rule-breakers are generally punished by simply being ignored by the rest of the clan, a horrifying prospect for the highly social Mbuti.

Night comes to the forest with a deafening eruption of katydids and crickets and the *gonk, gonk, gonk* of awakening banana bats. Farther off, the groans and screams of emerging nocturnal animals and reptiles reach the camp from deep within the jungle.

Around the community fire, meanwhile, the clan gorges itself on fresh-cooked bushbuck meat, passing around pot after pot of steaming ribs, shanks, and organs, each piece skewered with a bamboo stick and placed atop leaf plates. The Mbuti are convinced Karen's lock of hair played a role in the successful hunt and so they honor us with favored cuts: a bushbuck's heart and liver. We eat more meat that night than ever before in our lives, then quit to watch the Mbuti go on for another hour, their stomachs seemingly bottomless. The clan will eventually consume every last edible scrap of their catch over the next two days, following a custom of never killing a plant or animal without using it completely.

It's late when Karen and I crawl into a tiny guest hut that night, then listen as a nearby mother sings her baby to sleep, retelling in song the afternoon events of gathering and hunting. The next morning dawns warm and muggy and the circle of leafy huts are steaming from an early morning tropical rain shower. But the gaiety of the night before carries over. A father plays with his son, pretending to be an antelope while the child throws a fragment of hunting net over him. Everyone in camp roars with laughter at this.

It doesn't take a degree in anthropology to recognize people utterly content with their lives and their culture. So it's no mere lapse into noble-savage romanticism to call Mbuti society one of the best examples of group happiness the world has ever produced. Nor is it a stretch to say that this way of life, basically unchanged for many thousands of years, points out the way other hunter-gatherers of the tropical rain forests and around the world probably lived in prehistoric times. Most of them were surely content and happy and did not live, as usually imagined, in constant fear and danger.

Over a breakfast of still more bushbuck meat and a few boiled mushrooms, Ageronga explains to us that the Mbuti clan will occupy this camp for only a few months before moving on when the surrounding game and collectible foods begin to thin. The clan will travel ten or twenty miles in a new direction, then build all their chairs, tables, and houses in about an hour. The camp the Pygmies abandon will quickly return to jungle. The old huts, uncared for, will tumble. Vegetation will cover up the paths. The refuse heaps will rot and form good soil. Soon, to the unpracticed eye, there will be no evidence left at all that people had once joyfully lived here. Within a year or so, the wild game will return and mature and multiply and the edible fungi and fruits will reemerge in full. Mbuti people will eventually live here again, steeped in abundance.

Ageronga, Moko, and the others may rightfully be said to be a natural part of their environment. Their hunting methods never pose a threat to the survival of any species of animal. Indeed, no life form, flora, or fauna, has ever become extinct at the hands of African Pygmies. The harmony between people and place is total.

What a contrast with the BaBira people and other cultures the world over, including our own, which exploit the rain forest by means dramatically less intelligent. It is estimated that the tropical forests of Africa alone are disappearing at the rate of more than 4,500 square miles each year. We outsiders ask more of the forest than it can provide, just as we ask more of the planet as a whole than it can provide without dying in the process.

No wonder the Mbuti are content to stay where they are, resisting assimilation to life outside the forest, steadfastly embracing ancient ways free of the acquisitive western appetite for more and more things. It is the genius of the Mbuti that they understand what wealth is. They have a wealth of freedom. A wealth of leisure time to spend with family and friends. A wealth of good food and tools permanently available thanks to good stewardship. A wealth of community life, of song and dance. They are poor only in those feelings of alienation and incompleteness characteristic of modern people insulated from nature and one another by a cocoon of excess. More than a century ago, the British-American explorer Henry Morton Stanley thoughtlessly described the Mbuti as living "the life of human beasts in morass and fen." How comfortably that description now fits the modern, civilized world from which Stanley once hailed.

It's mid-morning when Moko stands and signals he's ready to guide us back to the BaBira village ten miles away. The Mbuti clan has insisted on loading us down with a gift of at least ten pounds of choice bushbuck steaks, wrapped in leaves and tied up with vines. It's now well past ten o'clock and none of the Mbuti are even thinking about work. After yesterday's success, there will be no need to hunt today, so beyond a few camp chores, everyone is free to relax around the fire, smoke tobacco, play with their children, bathe luxuriously at the nearby river.

Karen and I shoulder our packs, not quite ready to leave this remarkable place but respectful of the Mbuti desire to be left alone even as we thank them for the welcoming hospitality that embraced two complete strangers. As we plunge back into the forest, I pause for one final glimpse over my shoulder at the camp. My eyes rest on a young father sitting by the fire, his three-year-old son in his lap. The father quietly sings with his mouth up against the boy's ear. The words of the song are few. They simply say, "The forest is good. The forest is good."